You Can Take the Cat
Out of Slough . . .

Also by Chris Pascoe

A Cat Called Birmingham

About the author

Chris Pascoe lives in High Wycombe with his wife,
daughter and two cats (at the last count).
This is his second book.

You Can Take the Cat Out of Slough . . .

Chris Pascoe

First published in Great Britain in 2006 by Hodder & Stoughton
An Hachette Livre UK company

First published in paperback in 2007

1

A CIP catalogue record for this title is available from the British Library

ISBN 978 0 34089865 9

Typeset in MT Sabon by
Palimpsest Book Production Limited,
Grangemouth, Stirlingshire

Printed and bound by
Clays Ltd, St Ives plc

Hodder & Stoughton policy is to use papers that are natural, renewable
and recyclable products and made from wood grown in sustainable forests.
The logging and manufacturing processes are expected to conform to the
environmental regulations of the country of origin.

Hodder & Stoughton Ltd
338 Euston Road
London NW1 3BH

www.hodder.co.uk

To Lorraine and Maya

and

*to my mother, who hardly features in this book because
she does very little that could be deemed 'totally stupid'.
And to Dad, who does feature in this book.*

Contents

Introduction – the First Day   1

Test Your Cat's IQ   11

The Eagle Has Landed   17

Auto-Brumism   27

A Break with Brum   39

Sammy's Suicidal Shenanigans   49

View from a Kite   57

Mrs Chippy & Co.   61

The Bovine Tiger   71

Dave's Diary   79

More Cats Like Birmingham   91

Beggar, Billy, Barmy Spy   103

The Mousetrap   115

Marinating Rites   121

The Most Peculiar Case of the Seaside Village
    and Its Missing Cats   131

Skater Frog   137

The Missing Link   143

Gazebo!   155

Weird Pets   161

The Carpet-fitters   171

Death Threats   181

Epilogue   189

Introduction – the First Day

'*Genius may have its limitations, but stupidity is not thus handicapped.*'

Elbert Hubbard

L ast summer, I decided to do something monumentally stupid.

Which isn't especially strange in itself – I do something fairly idiotic most summers, just rarely with solid intent.

As stupid ideas go, this was a big one. I decided to stay at home with my two-and-a-half-year-old daughter Maya and disaster-prone tabby Birmingham, Brum for short. And also with Brum's rather vicious live-in partner, girl-cat Sammy, whom I intended mainly not to wake. Let biting cats lie.

Staying at home wasn't laziness on my part. It was all in the loose name of book research, although I have to admit that I thought that the plan, surprisingly endorsed by my wife Lorraine (with the strong proviso that I finally erect the gazebo I'd left rotting in the garage for three summers), was a dream ticket to half a year down Easy Street. No more between-writing projects and boring supplementary fill-in jobs for me. No more mind-numbing hours in that telephone call centre.

Just feet-up-at-home time, taking notes and enjoying quality time with Brum and Maya. Why I believed time with Brum would, with all the years of contrary evidence, be quality I'm not at all sure. I'm equally uncertain why I believed that looking after a toddler full time would be an 'absolute doddle'. I know Maya's day-nursery carers nicknamed her 'Duracell' and suggested she was a little over-boisterous, but why didn't I take notice of the haunted look in their eyes when they told me those things?

And, of course, there was a third reason for staying at home. It wasn't just research and skiving. There was a 'time running out' factor.

I wanted to spend a summer with my mad-toddler daughter

3

and catastrophic cat while I still could – an early summer in Maya's life, a late one in Brum's and, as I was soon to discover, a ridiculously embarrassing one in mine.

Because Maya won't be a toddler for very long, and I suppose that now Brum's coming up to fourteen years old, these would have to be classed as his winter years. I actually believe that spring, summer and autumn were all over in the first six months and the rest has been one long nuclear winter, but there you go. In cat years, he's now a recognised OAF.* The usual equation is one human year to seven cat years, which will make Brum ninety-eight this birthday. A few months after that, totally predictably on April Fool's Day, he will be one hundred years old.

How on earth has he managed to run up an innings like that? His survival strategy has been simple, straightforward and stupid. From the word go, he took on the persona of a rum-soaked blindfolded man and set off on a hundred-year stroll through a minefield. On he stumbled, crashing from one blast to the next, tabby fur flying here, whiskers and ear-tips blown sky high there, but it's worked – he's still with us.

And somehow he's managed to retain the scruffy look and exuberantly dangerous energy of a kitten. Sure, he's showing the odd signs of old age – he will suddenly sigh aloud for no apparent reason, for instance (not sure if this isn't wind). I also think he may be having 'senior moments' (but these differ so marginally from his usual moments that I can't be certain). He even falls asleep in mid-conversation (Brum, you're standing on my hand. Brum? Brum?) to awake confused and spluttering. But that's about it. In every other aspect, he's just as he was when he was naught but a youngster – perilously idiotic.

Thinking about it, you could actually have been describing Lorraine's seventy-something father back there, you really could . . . apart from the 'exuberantly dangerous kitten' bit. And Walt's not one for chasing mice either. Well, not so much since the hip replacement, anyway.

*Old Age Fur-ball.

There *is* one other giveaway to Brum's advancing years, and that's his absolute hatred of new technology. Maya and the microchip have brought an absolute deluge of automated, singing, dancing, interactive toys into his life.

Brum can't move a paw without coming face to face with plastic babies explaining that they want a dummy and calling him Mummy, barking metal dogs that run headlong at him, inanimate-looking objects that suddenly ask him what letter 'cat' begins with, turtles in shades that call him dude and implore him to 'climb on and ride surf' and, worst of all, even the floor itself holds surprises, especially in the form of a keyboard mat.

The keyboard mat is one of Maya's favourite toys. A ten-by-six sheet of plastic, it has piano keys down the middle and pictures of all manner of musical instruments around the sides. Each piano key plays a note when stepped upon and each musical instrument provides a short, loud tune.

When Brum first blundered on to this modern marvel, we were treated to the sight of a startled cat jumping two feet in the air to the beat of a bass drum, only to land to a trumpet fanfare and take off again, before racing up and down, round and round, without ever having the sense to leave the mat, and consequently thrashing out a fairly accurate piano rendition of the Sex Pistols' 'Pretty Vacant', complete with spiky-eared pogo dancing.

It's impossible to judge how long Brum has left in him. I've never once, during his entire life, given him more than a couple of weeks. Maximum. And I got a taster of life without Brum early this year when he decided to get suddenly, and very seriously, ill.

One moment he seemed perfectly OK, though vomiting a little more enthusiastically than usual, the next he got sick in remarkably dramatic style. No half-measures with this lad – he simply walked into the room, eyes blazing a shocking yellow, looked at us in what appeared to be total surprise and fell over sideways. He then lay on the floor making Tommy Cooper magic act guffaws and grunts, and seemed to pass out. Having total confidence in Brum's uncanny ability to survive absolutely anything and everything, I fully expected him to get up, bow and leave the room. He didn't. It suddenly occurred to me that it was round about time he dropped dead.

Which, it so happens, he'd almost done. He was rushed to the vet's where Commissioner Herbert* grudgingly admitted there might still be a chance for him. But, he advised, the cost would be high and his survival chances slim. Brum had some terrible liver complaint, he was jaundiced and getting weaker by the hour. But this was our Brum. You can't write him off over a thing like money, even if the final cost was near on seven hundred pounds (tabby bastard).

He spent three days on a drip, being pumped with all sorts of drugs and antibiotics, and at no time during the first two days did I think I'd be seeing him again. It suddenly hit me what life would be like without him. When I'd stopped grinning, I thought of the downside.

I realised that when Brum goes, there will be a void in my life that no other cat could possibly fill, because he isn't just a cat, or even just a clumsy, half-evolved creature vaguely resembling a cat. He's a good friend. Brum has been with me for almost a decade and a half. He's seen and survived every phase of my adult life – from sad singleton, through various doomed relationships and total humiliation during a year's stay on a farm, to my life-saving move into a house containing Lorraine and the snarling Sammy. Just when he thought things were finally settling down, along came the recklessly unpredictable Maya.

I began thinking maudlin thoughts, glancing at his food bowl and wishing I'd given him more of his prized tinned tuna and processed ham, staring at our living-room curtains and imagining never again seeing his pointy-eared silhouette fall off the outside wall.

But, of course, the little git came back, didn't he. Grinning like a lunatic, purring and demanding food, totally blasé about the fact he'd just cost us a small fortune.

---

*Our vet develops a nervous tic at the sight of Brum and me. It is very reminiscent of the near-nervous-breakdown reaction of the commissioner in Pink Panther movies (played by Herbert Lom) when dealing with Inspector Clouseau.

Which got me to thinking, I've hardly had an easy ride with *him*, have I?

A quick rundown of Brum's manifold history of disasters – regular fur fires averaging one case of self-induced inferno every two years, the riding and damaging of moving cars (as Maya's talking turtle would say, 'You have serious thrill issues, dude'), destruction of neighbourhood property while being beaten up by small birds, serial room wreckage and much, much more – suggests just how bad a ride it's been. And come to mention it – my life on the farm was only a total humiliation because he made it so. I didn't sit in a puddle of diluted cow's muck on a winter morning because it seemed like a splendid idea (that's a spring activity). No, it was because *he* sent me sprawling and *he* put me there – just as he's put me in most of the shit I've ever been in!

And age hasn't diminished Brum's scope for catastrophe either, as you'll discover in the pages of this book. If anything, I think he's trying to up the tempo.

No, we're definitely as bad as each other, he and I. But I have to admit that Brum's near-death episode, as much as anything else, pushed me into my monumentally thick decision to take Maya out of nursery and pack in the day job.

Perhaps not surprisingly, things didn't start well.

I awoke at 6.30 a.m. on that first day in late spring to the sound of Lorraine's alarm clock. I smiled a happy smile, knowing that its harsh beeping no longer applied to me. Then the gentle, hundred-decibel cries of 'MUMMY, DADDY, IS IT MORNING YET?' drowned out the alarm clock. *That* noise applied to me.

The moment Lorraine's car pulled out of the drive, I hit a major stumbling block. I had absolutely no idea what to do with Maya. It was a toddler, it was awake, and it was looking at me.

And then she was off: 0–60 in two seconds. Fifty events got under way instantaneously. Being male and therefore physically incapable of multi-tasking, I was immediately out of my depth. She's a concentration time bomb, you see. She has to be doing something new within five minutes of starting something new or she blows. Not wanting to blow the house up (and after a morning of Maya it looked very much as though the house *had* suffered a seriously explosive moment), and also noting that Brum wasn't entirely happy with our lingering presence, I decided to take her to the playground, where she could destroy some council property rather than mine.

I've always thought that playgrounds are great. It's somewhere Maya can get really excited and burn off some of that crazed energy of hers, and I can stare blankly into the middle distance. But the playground turned out to be the very reason things got off to a seriously bad start. First Maya ran off and I had to chase her all over the place, always three feet behind, always panting like an over-excited spaniel. Then she hurtled up a plank on to a slide-cum-assault-course, going over rather than around the toddlers already on it.

A particularly stern-looking couple whose offspring had just been squashed gave me a 'control your child' look, and I called out to Maya to do various things alien to her (wait your turn, be nice, don't jump on people's legs).

After about five minutes of constantly coaching Maya in etiquette, I seemed to gain the approval and respect of the stern-faced couple. But then, as Maya reached the top for the umpteenth time, she turned left and not right. Right was a slide, left appeared to be a sheer drop to the floor, and I suddenly realised that a vital couple of planks were missing. She was almost certainly about to drop seven feet to the ground. I lurched forward, shouting words such as BLAHHH and GNNNNERRR by way of explanation as I trampled over Stern Woman's feet and sent Stern Man sprawling backwards into a litter bin. They were impressed, I could tell.

Maya, bless her, merely glanced over the edge before I could get anywhere near her, turned and slid serenely down the slide, rendering my actions utterly incomprehensible. The stern-faced couple now looked a whole lot sterner and more than a little surprised. I was about to explain and apologise but Maya was now running off at Mach 1 and I had to go with her. You do apparently. As I legged it into the distance, I think I left them in no doubt as to where Maya gets her ways.

It wasn't a great outing for me. No more than twenty minutes later, already embarrassed enough for one day, a case of mistaken identity should have seen police officers rushing to the scene and making an instant arrest on the grounds of harassment. Luckily, the lady I harassed didn't send for them. As usual, I was the architect of my own downfall.

Shortly after Maya and I left the playground and zigzagged through mud puddles to the nearby banks of the River Thames armed with bread to throw at ducks' heads, I spotted an old friend of mine named Dulcie.

Dulcie works in a lingerie store. We go back a long way, decades in fact, and have a mocking, knockabout sort of relationship. So, assuming she was taking the scenic route to work and aiming a little risqué innuendo at her profession, I grinned broadly and called, 'ALRIGHT THERE? OFF TO SHIFT SOME PANTS, ARE YOU?'

Only it wasn't Dulcie. With hindsight, I should perhaps have waited until the woman got a little closer and had been one hundred per cent positively identified before making a remark so totally borderline. 'Off to shift some pants' is not your average way of greeting a total stranger in the park. She stopped sharply, glared at me and assertively dared me to repeat my remark. I stammered an uncomfortable apology, trying to explain what I'd meant and making things much worse with my mumbled comments about lingerie. I finally shut up, frowned and pushed Maya in front of me to show that I was a family sort of bloke and couldn't possibly have meant anything dodgy. And also to absorb any body blows.

The woman glared once more for good measure, looked pityingly at Maya and marched off down the footpath. I let out an audible 'phew' and she stopped dead in her tracks. I made absolutely sure I didn't breathe again until she was out of earshot.

Once again, I was left pondering the total unfairness of life. How dare Dulcie be the spitting image of this woman. Dulcie was in big trouble next time I saw her. Evil little clone.

All in all, then, quite a day to set the ball rolling. Harassment and assault. Not bad. The only really remarkable thing about the day was that Brum didn't catch fire. But there were still four or five months to go.

If I learnt nothing from my first ever day in full-time toddler-minding, and I certainly did learn nothing, I at least acquired an instant respect for all those looking after children everywhere, including Brum, who's still a babysitter at heart, running to Maya's side whenever she cries, despite the obvious dangers.

Childcare and tabby-watching proved ridiculously exhausting from day one, and life is just so much simpler and safer in a nice, safe office environment.

But, in the name of research, I'd made my decision. No safety for me. The foreseeable future lay with Brum and Maya, so safety wouldn't come into it.

I never had any doubt that the scope for disaster with all three of us at home was limitless. I just needed to keep taking those notes because without the disasters there's no material. So, convinced I had the right team in place, I sat back and waited with high expectations and, predictably, everything went completely wrong.

Perfect.

Test Your Cat's IQ

'The man is a wit and a half, but refuses to employ more than a third of it. The maths speaks for itself.'

Stephen Pusey

I often trawl the Internet for cat-related sites. I am not telling you this simply to reaffirm my 'saddo' status, but to bring to light a current trend for testing your cat's intelligence levels. There are now an absolute deluge of 'Cat IQ Tests' available on the Web, and so I thought I'd try a few on Brum. I suppose I could have guessed that the results would be less than encouraging, but the masochist in me insisted I give him a chance. To say I was 'asking for it' is an understatement.

I downloaded a suitable test and immediately disagreed with the opening statement: 'We sometimes take our cats for granted.'

No. We absolutely don't. You can take a goldfish for granted, or a hamster for granted, but not a cat. How can you possibly take for granted an animal that will rip up your curtains, flay your wallpaper and puke on your bed. You can't. Cats take us for granted, not the other way round. Cats walk all over us, and not only in a metaphorical sense. They do actually walk on us. If we're in the way, they just trounce straight over us as if we're not there. We are totally incidental to them. How taken for granted is that?

I got over my resentment and printed off a 'test card'. This card's purpose was to ascertain whether Brum was creative, or had more conventional intelligence. Creative as in artistic, rather than the ability to create carnage and chaos. The test card comprised two mirror-image ducks, one on the left and one on the right. The task was simple. Hold the card up to Brum, once an hour, and see which duck he sniffed. Persistently sniffing the left duck would denote creativity; persistently sniffing the right, conventional intelligence.

Brum sniffed between the ducks. A duck on either side, and

he sniffed the blank space between them. He seemed not to notice the ducks at all. Five attempts in five hours produced exactly the same result. Brilliant. There wasn't even an intelligence rating for a cat that missed the ducks completely.

Test one: Creative intelligence – nil. Conventional intelligence – nil.

Test two was an odd one. It involved training Brum to jump through a hoop. The premise was simple enough – hold 'his favourite treat' on one side of a twelve-inch-high hoop, and let him eat it only if he jumped straight through. Repeat hourly, until the cat jumps through the hoop every time.

Never has my arm ached so badly. I held that hoop out for ten minutes an hour, but all he did was stare at me, grinning that happy cat grin of his. Once he even lay down and went to sleep. On several occasions, I lifted him up and put him through the hoop to demonstrate what I was looking for, but this only served to annoy him. Finally, after five attempts and five hours, with the hoop now barely off the floor, he stepped halfway through and stopped. He had no intention of continuing. He was quite definitely showing me his full range of capabilities. The hoop was a symbolic cat-flap – and he was stuck in it.

Test two: Task/reward reasoning skills – nil. Memory – nil.

Test three's aim was to discover whether a cat has 'invertist tendencies'. It sounded the sort of thing he *would* have, but I decided I'd better find out what 'invertist' means before jumping to any conclusions.

Apparently it refers to the way your cat sees things. If your cat often rolls upside down to observe an object, then chances are he has invertist tendencies. Brum often rolls off chairs *while* observing objects, but I don't think that counts. The invertist cat rolls upside down because he can see objects more clearly by observing them the wrong way up.

The simple way of testing for invertism is to observe the way your cat watches TV. If he takes an interest in what's on the screen, chances are his vision is normal. If he takes no interest, but then suddenly does when the TV is turned upside down, it means he can relate to the topsy-turvy images and therefore has invertist tendencies. Brum takes no interest in TV at all, so I turned the TV upside down.

Unbelievably, Brum rolled upside down and watched it. What on earth does that mean? He rolled over with it. That doesn't denote anything. The TV was upside down, but so was he. He couldn't see it the right way up, or upside down. But he could see it when both he and the TV were upside down. This was pure nonsense. I checked the 'intelligence rating' notes. Nothing. What he'd done was unheard of. He'd gone off the scale again.

Test three: Invertist tendencies? No . . . just strange tendencies.

The final test was to assess a cat's ability to register two-dimensional patterns. The test card contained rows and rows of birds, with one rabbit hidden among them. I could hardly be bothered. There was no way he was going to spot the rabbit. I held the card up, somewhat nonchalantly, and waited for Brum to fail. His reaction was entirely unexpected. He attacked my hand.

Something in that pattern sent him doolally. He took one look and launched himself at me, grabbing my arm with all four paws and sinking his teeth into my fingers. I decided against showing him the card again.

So, an assessment of Brum's intelligence. He failed the first two tests with flying colours, and betrayed worryingly psychotic reactions during tests three and four. Going by the website's own rating system, my cat is an idiot.

The Eagle Has Landed

*'One flew east and one flew west, and one flew
over the cuckoo's nest.'*

Nursery Rhyme

As the summer got under way, it became patently clear that there was something wrong with it. It was the sun. It kept staying out. And as long as the sun stayed out, so too did Maya's paddling pool.

Maya is irrationally jealous about her paddling pool. I'm not allowed in it, Lorraine's not allowed in it, and Brum is most definitely absolutely certainly not allowed in it. The slightest nose-twitching tabby curiosity is met with a tantrum of terrifying force. In the light of this you'd think Brum would actively avoid diving head first into the thing, wouldn't you? But not our Brum.

Never has a garden item proved so much a centre of wet calamity. Three times in the first few weeks of summer I've watched him swimming around, albeit extremely unhappily, totally drenched within its plastic walls. On three further occasions he's squelched into the living room, dripping all over the carpet and sidling around Maya, so I'd say it's odds on he's taken unobserved dips too.

It's great, by the way, that he now aims for Maya when he's wet. He's spent a lifetime bounding happily from bath-drenching or rain-soaking to squelch down on *my* lap. So common were our joint drenchings that I eventually became immune to them. I'm not saying I evolved a duck-like feathery coat that repelled water, it's just that I stopped reacting in any significant way. I stopped yelling in surprise as he landed, stopped jumping up and down and swearing like a trooper as he tried to settle. I finally got so used to it all that I'd just robotically change my trousers without registering annoyance, or even hissing. I think this bothered Brum. I think he felt hurt that he wasn't getting due recognition for the gag. Maya's reaction, therefore, came as a breath of fresh air. It's just as mine used to be before I became boring.

As his thick wet fur slides along her jeans, she tries to move sideways away from him, shrieking with her hands in the air, but he slinks along with her. She tries to back up, but he then slips sideways, always rubbing his soaked fur against her legs and stomach as she waves her hands frantically and screams louder. The scene becomes reminiscent of a dramatic Spanish dance routine, the pair striding around the room in perfect unison, her hands appearing to be playing the castanets as she wails her tragic story (in this case the tragedy being that her jeans and T-shirt are getting very, very wet and, since giving up the Pampers, she's already had enough trouble with that particular issue, thank you very much) and Brum looking deadly serious, head held proudly in the air, the Latin dance partner to a tee.

Anyway, I reckon he's ended up in that pool at least six or seven times in four weeks. That's not normal, is it? That's not even just clumsy. Is there perhaps a tabby lodestone concealed within the pool's air chambers? Or are mer-cat sirens attempting to lure him to a watery grave with their irresistible moggy wailings? No – we must always remember that the word 'normal' doesn't apply in any 'normal' way when dealing with Brum. Six or seven pool dips in a month? Absolutely Brum-normal.

Brum's range of splashdown approaches has been varied and impressive, but I think for sheer surprise value his cat-flap approach stands out as something quite special. Brum's had a typically bad year, cat-flap-wise, and I really don't think he needed this. His cat-flap problems began, of course, the moment we had one installed. As time's gone by, his attempts to employ it as a legitimate door have progressed from an early hundred per cent failure rate to his experimenting with many different, and always doomed, approaches. At one time he even started climbing through backwards, which resulted only in the disturbing spectacle of a tabby rear end appearing from nowhere and wiggling at you for half an hour.

In the early spring, he developed a brand-new approach, which can only have been born of frustration. In total contrast to his usual nervy, one-paw-at-a-time bunch-up, he suddenly threw caution to the wind and just bowled himself head first at it. This only *almost* works.

Speaking in an aerodynamic sense, something is horribly wrong with Brum. He somehow manages to execute a magnificent back-flip as he flies through. It's spectacular. He'll hit the cat-flap with all four paws pointing down, but by the time he's through, they're all pointing in the air. It's the most incredible feat of high-speed, twisting gymnastics I've ever seen.

On an outbound trip, the brutal finale involves him sliding painfully along the patio on his back. Inward is more of an upside-down descent into Sammy's food bowl, which is only less painful if Sammy isn't eating at the time.

Because of its obvious flaws, he'd largely abandoned this 'raging bull' approach by the end of spring, but suddenly readopted it at the worst possible moment – on a day the cat-flap wasn't there any more.

We'd purchased new doors, you see. And also new front and rear cat-flaps, which we hadn't quite got round to installing when Brum came charging across the patio and threw himself head first at a solid wood door. Raging bull is spot on. He butted it so hard with the top of his head, sadly deficient in the horn department, that his rear legs lifted a foot off the ground. Wow, that must've hurt. He staggered backwards across the patio as if he'd just taken a fifteen-round pummelling from Tyson.

Maybe it could've happened to any cat; I don't know and seriously doubt it, but only Brum would retreat ten feet back and then come thundering back for another go.

I felt I should've been waving a red cloth and shouting 'Olé' (real Spanish feel to all this, isn't there?) rather than just jumping in front of him and sweeping him up out of harm's way, but a red cloth in front of a closed door wouldn't have been a 'fun thing'. Not for him, anyway.

The rear cat-flap got installed the following week, by which time he'd learnt his hard-knock lesson and got back to carefully blocking it with his body and irritating the queue (Sammy). If Brum had kept to this totally useless method of cat-flapping, he wouldn't have had to endure his cat-flap-cum-competition-diving event, but as always Brum's comic timing was impeccable.

When I fill Maya's paddling pool, I do it from a tap beside the back door which the hosepipe doesn't fit. I therefore fill it as much as possible under the tap and then move it to the centre of the patio before adding buckets of warm water from indoors. Unfortunately, filling the pool from the outdoor tap places most of it briefly outside the back door and, of course, just beneath the cat-flap.

Brum, as only Brum would, decided he was now entirely happy that the door was no longer a solid block of wood, and that today would be a great day to go for another good old-fashioned rhino charge.

Maya and I were watching the pool fill, her a demented mix of impatience and excitement, me holding her back with all my might, when out of nowhere a determined-looking Brum hurtled out of the cat-flap, did a mid-air flip on to his back, skimmed the surface of the water like a stone, reached the pool wall with his head and sank beneath the waves – also in a very stone-like manner.

For the briefest of moments, only his four legs protruded from the water as his back hit the bottom.

Maya and I stood in silence, our jaws dropping in unison.

Maya broke the silence with a roar of sheer, undiluted rage.

She was, without doubt, all ready to hold him under and punch his lights out. I held her back, not only to save my furry friend from a beating, but also because I knew that the next bit could be extremely dangerous. Brum has trouble getting back to his feet on dry land, never mind in twelve inches of cold water. The thrashing, splashing mayhem that ensues is painful enough to watch, but I've learnt from bitter experience that the pain's far worse if you try to lend a helping hand.

And so, I held back an enraged toddler, who angrily kicked and punched the air as Brum laboriously surfaced, spluttering and gasping for air. Eventually he was back on all fours and looking seriously irritated. I suppose he had every right to be. If I stepped out of my back door and fell straight into a pool of cold water, I suspect I'd probably be a mite peeved.

His eyes met mine and he instinctively knew I was in some way to blame. Of all the stupid places to put a bloody paddling pool. I swear he bared his teeth at me. He slid over the edge of the pool like a greased eel and wandered off across the patio, leaving a rather comical trail of wet paw-prints. As he reached the top of the garden, he stared down at me. Living as we do on the side of a steep hill, he was now two walls and fifteen feet above me, and for a moment I thought he was going to perform a mountain-lion-style pounce-and-kill manoeuvre, so annoyed did he look. But instead he gave a meek miaow and lay down to glare viciously and dry out in the warm sunshine.

A couple of minutes later, unbelievably, he was at it again, this time so blinded by out-and-out, all-consuming fear that it wasn't a case of the pool being a bad thing but rather the better option.

Something had just landed up there on the garden wall with him, something so unexpected, so terrifyingly out of the ordi-nary, that Brum actually shrieked in alarm as he came running full pelt down the garden steps, skidding round the corner without slowing, still looking over his shoulder as he hit the pool's plastic wall, briefly collapsing it and stumbling face first back into the water. My disbelieving laughter stuck in my throat, mainly because I'd just seen the thing he was running from.

As Brum thrashed around beneath my feet, gulping in huge mouthfuls of pool water and trying desperately not to die, I stared in awe at the eagle sitting at the top of my garden.

It stared back evilly, regarding me with an unblinking eye. Brum, meanwhile, finally found his feet, but this time didn't even attempt to leave the pool, instead standing stock still and joining in all the general staring going on. A sudden crescendo of pool bubbles confirmed he was every bit as edgy as me.

And so, a stand-off ensued, a huge eagle at the top of the garden, a man and a flatulent cat half submerged in a paddling pool at the bottom. The eagle shuffled on its feet. Brum and I tensed. At this point, Maya emerged through the back door from a toilet break. Her brow instantly furrowed as she spotted Brum back in her pool. Oh no! Sudden screams of outrage broke the tight silence, and bubbles rose once more as the startled eagle spread an absolutely enormous pair of wings and flew straight at us.

Brum ducked bravely beneath the water, and I grabbed Maya by the legs, making ready to swing her like a bat and strike the attacking eagle from the sky (not really – I grabbed her by the shoulders and pulled her into the considerable barricade of my solid six-pack waist . . . well, actually my 'wobbly two-pack with fifty per cent extra free'). The eagle swooped low. I fully expected Brum to be plucked from the pool and carried away to a mountain-top nest, but the eagle swept over our heads, close enough to cause a sharp down-draught, before nonchalantly gaining height and soaring away over the rooftops.

What the . . . ! I was stunned. So stunned I let go of Maya, whose concerns didn't involve giant birds of prey at all, but rather a pool-bathing cat who now had a whole new set of problems racing towards him. I acted quickly, scooping up Maya and running straight into a wall, before readjusting and making it through the door. I switched on Sky News, scanning the text for reports of zoo escapees. Nothing. How could an eagle have landed in my back garden and nobody be looking for it?

It had to have been an eagle. I'd never before seen a bird so impressive – that huge wingspan, that vicious-looking head, those beautiful red and black markings. I knew a retired neighbour to be very interested in birds. He spends hours staring at them through his big binoculars (at least, I hope that's what he uses them for), so if anybody could tell me why an eagle should be frightening cats into paddling pools in High Wycombe, he'd be the man. Maya and I set off down the road to see him, briefly passing a soaked Brum, who appeared to be muttering darkly to himself as he wandered off somewhere, no doubt to get a few more acts of dangerous stupidity in before teatime.

I rang Tom's bell and felt hopefully happy to see him answer the door with binoculars dangling from his neck. I asked whether he'd seen an eagle. Sort of inevitably, he laughed out loud. Tom's mirth, however, came not from the fact that I thought I'd seen an eagle, but that I hadn't seen one before. Apparently, the skies around us are full of them, and have been for at least a year. Only they aren't exactly eagles. I was perhaps getting a little carried away, but they're certainly impressively big birds of prey and more than a match for the sparrow-fearing Brum. They are actually red kites, released into the Chiltern hills a few years ago and now breeding like the rabbits they occasionally slaughter. What a great idea, I remarked, let's fill the local skies with whopping great sharp-clawed hawks for a laugh. Why not?

Tom was slightly taken aback by my attitude. He seemed to love these things, and couldn't believe my lack of enthusiasm. I then made a few comments about people interfering with nature. I'd really asked for it now. I was treated to this admonitory lecture that, leaving out the heartfelt comments on ignorant neighbours and unwanted observations on the continued lack of a gazebo in my back garden, reads like a red kite fact file:

1 Red kites are NICE. And you can stop giving me that doubtful look, young man.

2 They won't attack us but because they're big (two feet tall with a six-foot wingspan) and a bit vicious looking (they look mean, believe me) they've always had a bad press.

3 They used to be really common in Britain, but many farmers were wrongly convinced they killed sheep and ended up wiping them out in all but the central Welsh mountains, where sheep had greater worries on the ground. Big and formidable enough to convince people they killed sheep, eh? No wonder Brum dived like a fur-clad U-boat.

Walking back up the road, I glanced across the fields and immediately spotted two red kites hovering majestically in the distance. As I pointed them out to Maya, they were joined by a third. Maya laughed aloud and told me that I was being stupid. They were quite clearly birds, not kites. Stupid possibly, un-observant definitely. Our living-room window faces this field. How on earth had I failed to see birds with two-metre wingspans?

My only excuse is that the antics of two particular troublemakers occupy 99 per cent of my time and both involve looking down, rather than up.

Auto-Brumism

'If everyone hated you, you'd be paranoid too.'
D.J. Hicks

MRS L. J. PASCOE

RESULTS OF ALLERGY TESTING

Following extensive laboratory allergy testing, we can confirm
that you are allergic to the following substances / items:

Cats

Please do not hesitate to contact us should you have any
further queries.

Thus the summer deteriorated for my luckless feline friend. But it'd been coming for a while. For about the last five years, Lorraine has had an odd allergy. It involves an itchy face and hand rash and lots of amusing nasal-related fun, such as runny eyes and sneezing fits.

As I moved in about five years ago and have been responsible for the majority of bad things in Lorraine's life during the ensuing period, it was naturally assumed that the complaint was my doing. Whether I'd picked up deadly rural spores during my ill-fated farm days or was a major cause of stress-related illness was unclear. The untenable fact was that she was fine before I got there, and now she often wasn't. Brum, arriving with me, obviously wasn't the first cat to cohabit with Lorraine. It may have borne all the hallmarks of an allergy to his kind, but it obviously, absolutely wasn't.

It was.

Why the addition of Brum to the household should have triggered a long-dormant inflammatory condition hasn't been made at all clear. But then nothing has, really. It took the medical profession four years just to suggest an allergy test. Far be it from me to knock GPs and accuse them of merely grasping at straws rather than attempting to actually solve a problem, but not so far that I won't. GPs grasped at straws rather than attempting to actually solve a problem.

During the course of four years of regular visits, Lorraine was advised at different times to do each of the following:

- Change her brand of make-up
- Change her shampoos and bubble baths
- Give up alcohol
- Not change Maya's nappies (Thank you, thank you very much)
- Use about a dozen different prescription hand and face creams, including lethal-sounding lotions containing steroids and the like
- Steer clear of Maya's baby lotions, or possibly just steer clear of Maya

- Give up spicy food
- Give up alcohol this time, really
- Get me to change *my* shampoos, bubble bath and brands of make-up
- Change our heating system
- Thought we told you to give up alcohol
- Take up smoking so we can blame it on that
- etc, etc, etc.

Finally she had an allergy test and Brum and Sammy passed it. The result list covered three whole pages, completely blank but for the word 'cats'.

Not surprisingly, it was Brum who got the entire blame. Fair enough in a way, Sammy hadn't caused it before Brum's arrival. It was *him* again. On many occasions it's not so fair. Often Brum gets the sharp end of the stick where Sammy is concerned, simply because Sammy is elegant and shiny white and pretty and graceful and beautiful, and Brum is Brum. Tatty, spiky-haired little punk. Trailer trash to Sammy's upper-class society girl.

As a good example of this, I'll relate a visit to the vet's a couple of years back. Commissioner Herbert had 'gone away' for a while, I think to that place by the lake where everyone wears crisp white coats and nobody mentions long-haired tabbies.

I'd taken the two of them in for flu jabs and flea treatments. The new vet saw Sammy and went all soppy, crooning lines like 'Oh, now, she is beautiful, isn't she' and (tickling under the chin) 'Aren't you a lubbly liddle ting, then'. All this followed by a blunt, almost aggressive 'Right, put the other one on the table', and a quick stab in the back of the neck with a long needle. And then, bloody cheek, she said this, 'We've got a new anti-flea treatment you may be interested in. It's supposed to be marvellous. Only thing is, it's another injection and it's also pretty new and untested. You might want to try it on . . . that one . . . before giving it her.' I still can't believe to this day that she said that. In front of him as well.

Another case of this automatic Brumism came from a midwife-cum-health-visitor appointed to visit our home during the months following Maya's birth. She sat down on our sofa and went on for a couple of minutes about what a lovely cat Sammy was, totally ignoring Brum, who was sitting right in front of her and grinning like the Cheshire Cat.

She was the loveliest, smiliest, friendliest and most bumbling midwife I've ever met, and I've met two, but what (I think) she said next I must attribute either to my mishearing her or to her rapid regional accent.

She glanced at Brum and said, 'Scumrabbit.' It was said as one complete word, sort of quickly and angrily, and I had to rewind our conversation in an attempt to understand what she was saying. I couldn't understand. I still don't. At the time I smiled and said, 'Eh . . . sorry?'

Alas, the moment was gone and she was immediately rambling on about choking babies, or rather how to avoid choking babies . . . no, how to save babies from choking. Whatever she'd said, she'd certainly wiped the grin off Brum's face.

I'll carry on with Sue the Midwife for a few moments, because during the next half-hour she not only showed me how to save babies from choking, but a few pretty nasty kung fu moves to try on them as well.

Luckily, she demonstrated with a demo plastic doll and not a demo baby. While showing me how to take your choking baby and quickly lay it face down along your thigh, she slammed the poor doll's face straight into our heavy wooden coffee table. It looked very much like a trained lab technician skilfully dispatching a laboratory rat.[*]

In the shock of realisation that, technically, she had just demonstrated how to 'take the baby out' rather than save it, she brought her leg back up much too sharply, cracking her shin on the table and sending the doll hurtling into the air on the wrong end of a vicious drop-kick.

She completed the manoeuvre by screaming 'AAAAAiiiiii' in true Ninja style and grabbing her shin. The doll landed in our fireplace and it was all I could do not to stand and applaud.

The cats had already registered respect for her fighting skills by fleeing the room as the first attack went in on the doll. They'd seen enough by then to know she wasn't a midwife to mess with, especially as she'd already registered an abusive dislike of Brum.

Sue was so embarrassed by the time she left, I felt I'd better not ask why she'd called my cat a scumrabbit. It'd probably have been the straw that broke the midwife's back, so I left it at that and knew it was something we'd just have to live with.

---

[*]In case you don't know, by the way, a lab technician dispatches a rat in *exactly* the same manner Sue deals with a choking baby – smashes its head down so hard on the side of a hard surface that, in the rat's case, it's bye-bye and thanks for all the cheese.

I know this because a few years ago the subject featured on a radio show dealing with callers' most embarrassing moments. This particular chap, a lab technician, spent much of his working day 'preparing' rats for study in this way and had become cold and automatic in his actions. The embarrassing moment came when he visited his girlfriend's parents' home for the first time and, nervous and edgy, sat at the table making small talk and trying to be impressive and likeable. His girlfriend's young sister was happily playing with her hamster and plonked it on his sleeve. His mind far away, working out what to say next, he absent-mindedly picked up the hamster and slammed it down on the edge of the dining-room table. Still totally on autopilot, he then tossed it casually to one side and continued chatting, unaware of a problem until noticing the stunned faces of all around him.

I'd met Sue only once before, just before Maya was born, and on first shaking hands had been quite relieved. She was fun, pleasant and modern, unlike her predecessor, who'd probably started out delivering chipmunks on the Ark. We'd got used to the old one telling Lorraine such things as 'If Mummy's lucky after the birth, Daddy may treat her to a nice clay wrap to help her get her figure back' and, aside to me, 'They're a little expensive, Daddy, but you'll find they're worth splashing out on'. This despite the fact that Lorraine out-earns me to the degree . . . er, well, the degree someone with a proper job out-earns a grown man who watches cats fall over all day and takes notes, in fact.

After the well-meaning and efficient but ancient-attituded original, it was refreshing to meet somebody like Sue, even if she'd proved her talent for the ridiculous within ten minutes. You see, the baby-fighting incident wasn't her first embarrassment of this nature. Upon that first handshake she'd proceeded to get on with her evening's work, which on the surface appeared to be thoroughly terrifying ten mothers-to-be-any-minute-now and to cause ten already terrified husbands and partners to run for the vomitariums but was, in reality, lecturing a pre-natal class at High Wycombe Hospital.

After opening with a few happy sing-song lines about how unimaginably horrific and painful childbirth is, she attempted to run a video of a woman giving birth. Unfortunately she had no idea how to work the VCR and spent a few minutes muttering and giggling nervously as she tried to rewind the tape. She finally had to settle for a slow rewind with a picture on the screen, and left the room to get some notes while the tape made its laborious way back. The result was that her entire audience sat and stared in horrified silence, forced to watch as a red and blotchy baby was hurriedly pushed back into a screaming woman's vagina. I don't know about everybody else in that room but it certainly left me emotionally scarred, I can tell you.

Back to the point – Lorraine's allergic to Brum. Maybe most people are, which would cast light on the aforementioned instant dislike some seem to display towards him. Brum therefore had more setbacks to deal with, in the form of sanctions brought to bear against both himself and Sammy, namely being banned from our bedroom and not allowed to sit on Lorraine's lap, not that they often did for long anyway – the constant sneezing irritated them beyond belief.

The scumrabbit and his mate should have accepted that. Had Lorraine not been a cat-lover and miacis fancier,[*] she might well have made things an awful lot worse for the pair of them. They could have been respectfully asked to leave, for instance. Or banned from the house and forced to live on the streets with a gang of hard-nosed ferals in bowler hats and the like.

But did they accept it? Of course not.

Not for the first time, the cats declared a state of open rebellion. It was them against us. Two tiny fluffy felines against two big strapping humans. We didn't stand a chance.

The thing to remember in a war with cats is that they fight nasty. Not 'burning effigies of us in the street while all the neighbours look on' nasty, but nasty nevertheless (having said that . . . no, no, it couldn't have been them). Our massive advantages in air power (five feet taller than them), military might (twelve stone heavier than them – no, for pity's sake, I know, Lorraine, not in your case. Strewth) and strategic know-how (a brain over double the size that we use only half of) counted for absolutely nothing against their furry guerrilla tactics. We could keep closing the bedroom door but we'd always forget, just for a second, and they'd be in there like a shot. As the infamous saying almost goes . . . cats only need to get lucky once.

The area outside the closed bedroom door became no man's land. The minute we were out of sight they were busy, raking the door and ripping up the carpet in a frenzied attempt to burrow under it or maybe even dig trenches. It soon became apparent that

[*] The miacis lived millions of years ago, and scientists consider it to be the earliest known link to present day cats. Unlike modern cats, the miacis was cumbersome, clumsy and extremely thick. I therefore hold the firm opinion that Brum's links are stronger than most.

we were in a 'destroy the house to save it' situation. We were in trouble. We needed help. Cometh the Ice-toddler. Cometh Maya.

Maya – twenty-two pounds of manic cat-lover.

Maya – whose gentle strokes amount to club-fisted poundings, reminiscent of something animal rights protesters present as video evidence.

Maya – who loves Brum and Sammy so much she could hug them to death, and probably will.

Maya's main weapon was reputation. The cats' healthy respect for her, bordering on fear, gave her an edge that we, who get no respect whatsoever, couldn't hope to match. But how to get the largely neutral Maya into the war?

Easy. Tell her she's your little helper. She wants to help with everything. If you're tidying up she helps by emptying bins all over the carpet; if you're making the beds she'll strip them for you. But she really *does* want to help, she's just heavy handed. And heavy handed was exactly what was required here.

We told her the cats weren't allowed in Mummy and Daddy's bedroom and settled back to watch the carnage.

Zero tolerance would be an understatement. For the first time I saw in Maya the dubious qualities of the Hitler Youth. Her energy in carrying out her pedantic task was breathtaking.

Wherever the cats went she went. She stalked them like their shadows. She knew exactly what they were up to at all times, and reported back to us in detail.

'Brummy's eat Sammy's dinner.'

'Sammy hit Brummy with its claws.'

'Brummy's done a sick in your shoe, Daddy.'

And if they so much as dared walk towards the bedroom door, she was at them, whooping and screaming, arms flaying about like a demented chimpanzee, chasing them all the way to the cat-flap, which Sammy was able to escape through with rather more ease than Brum. She even extended her area of jurisdiction to the kitchen work surfaces and her own bed, protecting everything with a crazed passion and glee.

The result of her relentless onslaught was that Brum was soon able to claim one hundred per cent consistency in all wars fought. Total, utter, wretched defeat and disaster.

Despite a formidable ally in Sammy, he'd found no recourse but persistent retreat, and also found to his cost that Sammy was much better at retreating than he was, leaving him to fight every rearguard action, i.e. having his tail hauled back by a jeering toddler and getting his front end batted around by Sammy in all the excitement. Shot by both sides.

What really worries me about all this is – what if the doctors got it wrong? I know it's unthinkable that the medical profession could have made a mistake but consider this . . . it takes seven years to train a vet, and only five to train a doctor.

Bearing this in mind, we have to draw the conclusion that vets are almost fifty per cent better trained than doctors and therefore, medically speaking, we humans are treated worse than dogs. Of course, you could bring sensible arguments into it, like the fact that animals can't tell you what's wrong so those extra two years are all about the extra skills needed in diagnosis, but why on earth would we want to do that?

Whether fought for valid reasons, or just for fun, the war drew to a close. Brum, who expects to lose every campaign he enters, accepted the new regime with resigned subservience. But for Sammy, the sheer indignation of being beaten by a jeering toddler was a little too much to stomach. For almost two weeks Sammy refused to enter the house, banishing herself to the back garden and systematically unleashing an onslaught the likes of which the bird and rodent world had never seen.

'Shame she hasn't got a gazebo out there for a bit of shelter,' observed Lorraine.

One war was over, but another raged on.

A Break with Brum

*'Why is it that wherever I go, the resident
idiot heads straight for me?'*

Gwyn Thomas

Tired and edgy? Under intense pressure? Feel you need to get away from it all for a few days? How about a weekend break with Brum? That should finish you off.

When an old friend of Lorraine's confided in her that life was getting on top of her, Lorraine inexplicably reasoned that a few days in our company might help matters. And so it was that Cheryl arrived on our doorstep, travel-bag in hand, one Friday lunchtime.

Had Lorraine been at home to greet her, I feel quite sure that this poor woman, already in a state of tired, nervous disillusionment, would've probably had quite a pleasant start to her long weekend. But Lorraine wasn't at home. Lorraine had been forced to work (her bosses are always forcing her to work) on her planned afternoon off, mainly because of dark and menacing events suddenly unfolding at the Slough office (somebody had been caught smiling and so taken for tests). As it was, the door was answered by a man grinning disturbingly, a scruffy, worried-looking tabby cat and a wildly babbling toddler. In the background a white cat glared in narrow-eyed hatred and sharpened its claws threateningly.

Cheryl smiled and in my haste to make her feel welcome I hauled her through the door by her travel-bag. Assuming she would let go at some point I then dragged her a few feet down the hall. It was about then that I realised she really didn't want me to carry her bag. The problem seemed to be that she didn't know who we were.

I'd never met Cheryl before. She's from up in the grim dark North, and until now only a crackling second-hand voice on the phone. She knew of me, and she knew of Maya, but she also had

41

the wrong house number written down. When she'd knocked five doors down, therefore, and been told by the residents they'd never heard of us, she started systematically working her way up the street, calling at four empty houses before being wrenched bodily through the door of the fifth.

Everybody stopped. She asked whether I was Chris, and relaxed greatly when I confirmed I was. I showed her to her room, my back-bedroom office, and went off to make her a cup of tea, calling to her to make herself at home in the lounge whenever she was ready.

A few minutes later, I walked into the living room, two cups of tea in hand and Maya at my side, to find Cheryl's face contorted in terror. The cause of her discomfort was quite clearly the dirty great tabby sitting on her lap and leering straight into her face, his purr sounding off like a pneumatic drill. The farther Cheryl craned her neck back and away from her new friend, the farther he pushed his face into hers. By the time I'd put the cups down and grabbed him, he was near rubbing noses with her.

I pulled Brum away. The sound of tearing fabric wasn't encouraging. Neither was the fact that Cheryl appeared to be coming with us. I tried to lever Brum away at a steeper angle, but his claws were quite clearly hooked firmly into her silky top.

A further ripping noise prompted me to gently edge Brum back towards her, and our cat-sandwich trio moved as one down to the sofa.

'Can you get it off,' she said, with a distaste normally reserved for something stuck to the bottom of your shoe, 'I really don't like cats.'

'Yeah, I'm trying to,' I assured her, wondering whether she'd thought my first attempt was part of some dance routine Brum and I performed with all new guests, 'but his claws are stuck in your shirt. Can you try and unhook him?'

A few tentative stabs at Brum's paws told me she couldn't. Brum, whose purring still reverberated around the room, began trying to kiss her.

Maya felt the need to exert some sensible authority at this point, grabbing Brum's tail, screaming 'GET DOWN, CAT' and yanking hard. This had three immediate effects. One was the hunching of Brum's shoulders, another was the stubborn tightening of his grip and the third was another healthy r-i-p-p-p.

Cheryl gave up trying to poke Brum's paws into submission and began to panic.

'Get it off me, please, get it off!'

I moved on to the chair and began carefully extracting Brum's claws from her shirt. The first paw came free easily enough, but I then noticed with some alarm that the other had not only made a total mess of the nice silk shirt but somehow hooked itself into the bra behind.

'I think you need to help me here . . .' I started to say.

'GET IT OFF ME, GET IT OFF ME!'

And so it was that within five minutes of meeting Lorraine's oldest and dearest friend, Brum was ripping her shirt to bits and I was twanging her bra strap.

She'd have been better off moving in with a band of woman-curious, lust-crazed hillbillies.

I really hoped things would improve after a change of shirt. But as we sat sipping tea and watching *Bob the Builder*, Cheryl showed few signs of friendliness. In fact she didn't seem to want to talk at all. I glanced at the clock. Lorraine wasn't due home for three hours. It was going to be a very long afternoon.

As we sat in silence, Brum appeared in front of the lounge window. He sat on his wall and stared in at Cheryl. I could sense her flinch at the sight of him. We sipped tea in silence. Bob the Builder sipped tea on TV. Maya sipped milk and muttered something about bricks and mortar and getting the flipping pointing right. Brum carried on staring at Cheryl. Something in her seemed to snap.

'Does he have to sit there, just looking at me like that?' Cheryl exploded, the sudden broken silence making Maya spill her milk and tut loudly.

I apologised for him, adding that he was staring only because he was interested in her, which seeing as he'd just ripped the shirt off her back was probably already established. I got up to move him, and headed for the front door. As I opened it, it was Brum's turn to jump. So consumed had he been in Cheryl-study he hadn't seen me coming. It's never a good idea to make that clumsy idiot jump on a six-inch surface and, just for a change, he slipped backwards off the wall, a hurt and accusing glance and a pointed paw his last contact with me before his descent into the undergrowth. I watched him emerge with half a bush stuck to his head, and shut the door.

'There, that shifted him,' I announced as I walked back into the house.

I was amazed to see Cheryl laughing. Brum had worked his old magic. Had he fallen off the wall just to impress her? The old charmer. It might have taken another cat-life to do it, but he'd finally put her at ease. We chatted for half an hour and then Cheryl asked whether it'd be OK to have a shower before Lorraine got home.

Not owning a shower and not wanting to get the hosepipe out, I suggested she take a bath. Off she went and Maya and I settled down for a deadly round of Hungry Hippos, a game involving a bunch of huge, chomping hippopotamus heads, which Maya says look just like me, catching marbles in their mouths. The game usually descends into chaos and violence, but we both tend to enjoy it.

After three thrilling bouts Maya began blatantly cheating, and so I went off in a huff to make another cup of tea. No sooner had I left the kitchen clasping my hot drink than Cheryl began screaming blue murder in the bathroom.

I rushed to the door in alarm.

'Are you OK . . . Cheryl, Cheryl?'

'ARRGH, GET OFF ME, GET OFF!'

What on earth was going on in there! In sheer panic, and without a sensible thought in my head, I started to open the lockless door. NO! I couldn't do that. She was in the bath. Presumably without clothes on. I'd be in huge trouble.

She screamed again and there was much wild splashing.

With mounting concern. I pushed the door farther but then lost my bottle, just as she yelled, 'WHAT THE F*** IS THE F****** MATTER WITH THIS F****** CAT!' I instantly slammed the door shut, but not before losing hold of my tea-mug. To all intents and purposes it must have looked as though I'd shoved open the door, lobbed a hot-tea hand grenade into the room and slammed the door to deflect the explosion.

Whatever Brum was doing in there, I could only have made things worse.

Suddenly the door burst open and a towel-draped Cheryl brushed past me and into her bedroom. She slammed the door behind her.

I cautiously glanced into the bathroom. Apart from a floor covered in water and steaming tea, nothing looked amiss. I stepped inside. In the corner sat a smug tabby, casually washing and preening. I stared long and hard at him. Eventually he looked at me, in a casual 'What?' kind of way, performed the feline equivalent of a raised-eyebrow smirk and trotted past me into the hall.

I studied the room for a clue to what might have happened here. By the amount of garden greenery beside the toilet, I immediately guessed that this had been Brum's retreat following his earlier wall-fall. He's pretty well hidden down there. Cheryl got in the bath without realising she shared the room with her new-found arch enemy.

I shrugged. There were no further clues. I'd come up against a bathroom wall of silence. All I could be sure of was that it all ended with a tea grenade. I'd have to remember that. If, by some strange quirk of fate, I ever again needed to settle a dispute between a bathing woman and a slightly stupid cat . . . the best solution – chuck a cup of tea at them.

Cheryl eventually emerged from her room and asked for a plaster, explaining that Brum had launched on to the side of the bath, seemingly from nowhere, and indulged in a little toe fishing.

He's done this to me before and it's not nice. He spots your big toe in the water and claws it. You pull your toe away and he tries to reel it in by tickling your leg. Every now and then (although thankfully not this time) he leans too far forward and joins you in the bath.

It was a while before a clean but bloodied Cheryl rejoined us in the lounge. Brum was nowhere to be seen, but he somehow had a 'presence'. Cheryl twitched and reacted to every single noise in the house. It was as if an unseen Brum was even more dangerous than a visible one. As they say – keep your friends close, and your felines closer.

But Brum didn't suddenly materialise from the shadows. He was out for the next couple of hours. Somebody, somewhere might have seen a ridiculous accident that afternoon, but it wasn't us.

No, our afternoon went well. Maya and Cheryl became firm friends and even Sammy took a break from doing nothing to say a guarded hello, and Sammy at least has the social graces to say hello without shredding your clothing and cutting your toes. When not confronted with a frenziedly friendly tabby, Cheryl was quite an easy person to get on with.

Lorraine eventually arrived home and we all went out for a meal at a local pub. Things were good. We came home and Lorraine and Cheryl settled in the lounge for a chat while I put the coffee on.

There is definitely a hot drink connection to all this, because when I walked back into the lounge I was greeted by a huge, graunching crash followed by an avalanche. I stared in horror at a point just above Cheryl's head. Cheryl looked up, but too late. Instantly, she was battered by an absolute deluge of ornamental cats.

As bone-china Burmese and terracotta

46

tortoiseshells rained down upon her head they were quickly followed by a wooden shelf and a screaming Brum.

The shelf missed her left ear by three inches, cracking her across the skull. Brum and the shelf came as a package and he enjoyed a brief and impromptu game of 'head seesaw' before catapulting to the floor and scurrying round my legs in a bid to escape.

Lorraine rushed to Cheryl's aid. She seemed unhurt, if rubbing her head quite vigorously. I set down my tray and went after Brum. He and I were having it out this time. He'd personally seen to it that our guest's first day was a nightmare. He'd 'set about' her from the moment she walked through the door. Not content with damaging her clothing, attacking her feet and ruining her bath, he'd now collapsed a wall shelf on her head. That bloody little scumrabbit was quite definitely for it.

He'd gone, though. I don't know how much force he'd hit the cat-flap with, but it was still swinging wildly. I contented myself with the knowledge that with a launch of that velocity, he'd have skidded at least two feet on his back and hit the outside wall like a bullet.

Perfect retribution.

Over the next three days, I made great efforts to keep Brum away from Cheryl. With the levels of assault he'd achieved on day one, his only way of peaking would have been to kill her, and I definitely don't think that would've improved her mood.

But Brum kept trying to reach Cheryl, and somehow Cheryl warmed to Brum, as most people (with the possible exception of a few embittered health workers) seem to do. In fact, on the day she left she actively sought him out to say goodbye.

She found him on the front wall and held out a hand to stroke his head. Brum pressed his head into her palm in sheer delight and very nearly lost his balance again. Three pairs of hands reached out to steady him, and a brief, panicking-cat mêlée ensued. Shaken, hair on end, but trying desperately to remain cool in front of his new friend, Brum finally resumed his fond farewells. He lingered on the wall for some time afterwards, watching Cheryl drive away into the distance.

Later she sent Lorraine an e-mail, thanking her for the weekend and saying she'd had a good time, while agreeing wholeheartedly that it was indeed a shame that they hadn't had a gazebo to sit out in. She closed with the words, 'Isn't Brum great? What a little nutter. He really cheered me up!'

It would seem Brum has his uses after all.

Sammy's Suicidal Shenanigans

'Oh Woman! in our hours of ease,
Uncertain, coy and hard to please,
When pain and anguish wring the brow
An even greater nuisance thou'

Adaptation of a Sir Walter Scott poem

In a year devoted solely to swelling Commissioner Herbert's bank account, Sammy completely forgot her graceful, sleek and faultless status as 'feline proper' and fell off Brum's wall. No falling with style for Sammy. No happy landings or surfing opportunities. None of that old nonsense – just PLOP, CRUNCH.

At least, that's what we think happened. Another Brum requisite of great falling, of course, is to be observed doing it by a number of stunned people and to injure as many of them as possible. Sammy completely failed to observe even these traditions. This was absolutely not a stylish fall. Our only clue that anything had happened at all was a wounded Sammy crawling in, dragging a limp hind leg and complaining bitterly.

Our initial guess was that she'd been hit by a car, but our delighted vet assured us that her injuries proved much more 'consistent with a *really* nasty fall'. We were then asked whether she 'tends to climb trees' or whether we had 'any high walls around us'. High walls. The silly moggy had definitely fallen off Brum's wall, hadn't she? Five years of watching Brum's death-defying leaps into oblivion without him getting so much as a scratch had obviously turned her head. She'd decided to have a go, and instantly broken a leg.

I left her with the commissioner and headed home, seriously wondering whether Brum's anti-cat gene might be catching. For a few minutes I actually wondered whether Sammy was more like Brum than we'd realised.

I walked into the house and found Brum sitting in his food bowl.

Moments later he turned himself the right way round and began eating. Another moment passed before he sneezed loudly, sending an explosion of food in all directions. He looked up at me briefly, his face smothered in meat and jelly. No . . . she's nothing at all like him. Nobody is. Nobody alive, anyway.

A broken leg led to a nightmare situation for Sammy. After her incredibly expensive operation (my unfathomable decision to forgo pet insurance, even with a cat like Brum bumbling about the house, had proved another financial master stroke) Sammy was confined to a cage. Commissioner Herbert insisted on it. Had it been Brum he was treating, I'd have been deeply suspicious that he'd instructed us to put Brum in a cage purely out of spite, but we knew of no feud with Sammy so we did as asked. It was essential she kept still – no jumping, no running, no sword juggling, no walking even, for five weeks. Maya lent Sammy her old playpen and, with a little modification, it served the purpose.

Poor Sammy. Poor claustrophobic Sammy, who has a very good excuse for her hissy fits. She came from a broken home. The first home, that is. She broke the second one. That first home was a nightmare and involved beatings and imprisonment in dark cupboards. Now, we'd all like to give Sammy a good cuff round the ear but decent people restrain themselves.

The dark cupboards having left her deeply afraid of confinement of any kind, being locked in a barred cage for five weeks had to be about the harshest case of 'facing your fears head on' therapy possible. A bit like becoming a deep-sea diver to ease a dread of water.

And of course, her detention coinciding with me being at home for the summer, Sammy fully blamed her predicament on my wicked presence. In fact, as the household's official administerer of all cat medicines and receiver of multiple flesh wounds for my trouble, this was hardly the first time my relationship with Sammy had gone through the floor for health-related reasons.

Our opening medicinal clash had centred on an ear infection. Just when Sammy was showing indications that she might allow me to stay in her house (she hissed at me only on one in five meetings – an all-time low) I suddenly picked her up, mumbling soothing words that must have sounded deranged in the light of what was happening, pinned her to the sofa and squirted a jet of liquid straight into her ear. All this rather displeased her. Especially as my sudden odd behaviour became, necessarily, a serial habit. Three times a day, which was more or less every time I saw her, I'd chase her round the room, corner her, grab her and fire streams of cold gunge into her ear. She took it all well, hurriedly removing the skin from my face and hands and inflicting bite wounds a pit-bull terrier would've been proud of.

All in all a good little bonding exercise. I may have to think about producing a helpful pamphlet on my experiences, 'How to gain your cat's trust and lose a pint of blood a day – an easy-step guide'.

And after all that nonsense – now this. Now I'd locked her in a cage in the kitchen, her cat basket in one corner, her litter tray in the other, and bars all around her.

Even worse were the visiting hours.

Every time she looked up either a big daft and totally fascinated tabby face gazed in, or an excited toddler pushed unwanted toys and presents through her prison bars (all had to be first checked for saws, files and contraband catnip, of course). And, worst of all, twice a day I'd lift her out and push a selection of foul-tasting tablets into her mouth. She was deliriously happy, I can tell you.

Then, something else went wrong with her. Her breathing became erratic and harsh. Back to the commissioner, who was now taking a higher percentage of our earnings than the taxman, and who now diagnosed her as having unrelated lung problems and prescribed a course of steroids.

It was my turn to feel unsettled. This already big, strong, super-fecund* bitch-cat whose claw patterns were now indelibly etched on the backs of my hands and whose full dental records could be studied on my wrists was going on a course of steroids just at a time when she had a major issue with me. The last thing I

---

*I love this word. It suggests self-replicating, invincible, superhero powers and strikes fear into the heart: 'SAMMY, SUPER-FECUND SHE-MONSTER'. I found it on a cat-fact website and it actually applies to all female cats. It simply means that each of the kittens in a litter may have different fathers, which is pretty amazing in itself really – your twin may be your half-brother.

needed was a steroid-enhanced-pumped-up-muscle-Sammy coming out of that cage in a few weeks' time.

To accentuate my feelings of unease, something odd began happening almost as soon as the first steroid passed between her snapping teeth (along with an antibiotic and one or two thousand painkillers).

Having taken her pills, she settled back into her basket, there being little else to do in a six-by-five cage. Normal enough, but then she started purring loudly. So loudly that Brum, idly watching her every movement, was quite taken aback. His ears went back, his eyes became huge green saucers, his hackles rose and he edged out of the room.

He'd never heard anything like it from her, you see. Sammy never, ever purrs. She's far too cool for that sort of thing, and she'd really hate us to think she was happy about anything.

And here she was, purring so loudly she was creating an echo. It was most peculiar. She also appeared to be grinning in a very Brum-like manner, eyes closed, mouth turned right up at the edges in a look of sheer blissful contentment. I watched her in awe for a few minutes and grabbed the steroid bottle, checking its label and sniffing it for signs of Class A narcotics. After a while I shrugged, gave up trying to guess what was going on and went to get her some munchies.

This most un-Sammyesque behaviour continued for weeks, even after the steroids ran out (although she was a bit grumpy on the way down for a day or two). For the rest of her sentence she let me administer her painkillers without a bloodbath and even let Maya stroke her through the bars of her cage.

I couldn't help thinking it was a ploy. She was looking for early release, and as soon as she got out, she'd kill us. Especially me, whom she'd probably kill a few times. But on that happy day that the cage became a playpen once more, Sammy lay in her basket and grinned at us all in the same merry manner. After a couple of smiley days, we realised she had no intention of getting up.

The basket lay in exactly the same place as it had done within her prison, and her litter tray was still near by. Like some of her equivalent prison inmates in the human world, she'd become happy where she was and didn't want to be released. The 'facing your fears' therapy had worked. Her claustrophobia was cured. She now had agoraphobia.

We considered there to be every chance she'd reoffend just to get her cage back and as, in her case, reoffending meant plunging over a twenty-foot wall, we left her to her own devices and let her adjust to freedom in her own time. She gradually came out of it, slowly got used to walking around the house, eventually made her way through the cat-flap. And there was a bonus. That steroid reaction didn't go away. She was suddenly a much happier and far better-balanced cat. Why locking her up and pushing horrible things in her mouth should have cured a lifetime of neurosis I have no idea, but she's developed a cheerful confidence about her that had never been there before.

The greatest indication that Sammy has now, more or less, recovered from her early life traumas is a game she's started playing with Maya – hide and seek.

And they really do play this game properly. First Maya will hide and Sammy will stalk the house until she finds her. Maya isn't too hot at the game really, not yet understanding that clamping your eyes shut doesn't necessarily make you invisible, and so standing in the middle of the living room isn't technically hiding. As soon as Sammy finds her, usually within a couple of milliseconds, she herself hurries off to hide.

No longer does Sammy fear dark spaces. She actively seeks them out and waits patiently for Maya to find her in them. Maya strolls around the house repeating, 'Now, where's Sammy gone,' and Sammy waits with glee to be discovered. She is so good at hiding that Maya shouldn't really have a cat-in-hiding's chance of finding her.

It's the purring that gives her away.

View from a Kite

*'More people know Tom Fool than
Tom Fool knows.'*

Seventeenth-century proverb

S oaring through the skies, I can see for miles. I see trees, I see fields. A green, quiet world below me. Behind me my home in the highest trees and before me the noise and chaos of the town. I glide on the wind, through the blue sky, surveying the ground far below. The same wind ruffles my feathers, fills my consciousness with its buffeting, soothing rhythms. I see a shape below, a familiar shape on the edge of the town. I have seen this creature before. It's eyes are as mine – the eyes of a hunter – yet its movements are of fattened prey. I feel a kinship with the beast. Surely at some forgotten time our races were one, and yet, as I have progressed to become what I am, this thing has become a wall dweller, its only purpose to balance, badly, upon its dwelling. I swoop low, we exchange glances, at one with one another for the briefest of moments, an understanding of all things natural and beautiful passing between us in that instant. It staggers backwards. It looks surprised. It falls from its wall . . . again.

Time passes. Days, weeks. The seasons change. I hover high and watch my world. I watch for the creature, my wall-dwelling cousin. A connection has been made. It is time to meet, to reach out and know my kin.

I see him far below. My heart beating with anticipation, I swoop from the sky, diving as I would to kill, but there will be no killing today. I land suddenly beside the creature. His coat is wet. Is he also a creature of the water? His eyes widen in . . . what? Recognition?

No, terror. Shock and frenzied terror. As sudden as our meeting is his maddened departure. He is screeching, running on four legs, moving faster than I believed his clumsy body would allow . . .

Ah, I see he *is* a creature of the water.

Mrs Chippy & Co.

'Stubborn, fearless?
Call it what you will,
A cat may climb the mainmast,
But ne'er against his will'

Little Jimmy Daley

A glance through the annals of history throws up many great human names from the fields of exploration, science and heroism. Surprisingly, it throws up the odd cat as well.

Actually, when you stop to think about it, that shouldn't be so surprising. Cats have lived with us as companions for at least seven thousand years, ever since they moved in with our ancient ancestors to protect their grain from rodents. Now, cats don't lend themselves to heroism as easily as dogs or dolphins, mainly because they can't be bothered, but in all that time one or two cats should reasonably be expected to have left their mark. And they certainly have.

Simon of the Royal Navy is one such hairy hero. Simon was a black-and-white tomcat, drafted aboard the HMS *Amethyst* in the late 1940s. His job, the job of many shipboard cats throughout history, was to kill mice and rats. As is the knack of cats, Simon managed to ingratiate himself, no doubt through much leg-brushing and over-the-top feline friendliness, with the ship's captain. So much so that he got use of the captain's bed by day, and even slept curled up in his officer's cap at night. I would not often compare our Brum to such a cat, because Simon was an expert mouser and an all-round proper feline. But what happened to him one day in China is very Brum-like.

It was during the Chinese communist uprising. The neutral HMS *Amethyst* was on routine patrol down the Yangtze river, when a jolly communist battery decided they'd try to sink her for a laugh. Simon lay blissfully snoring on the captain's bed when a missile came screaming straight through the cabin wall and blew his bedroom to pieces. With eyebrows heat-shrivelled and whiskers burnt off, a dazed Simon stumbled on to deck coughing and spluttering and wondering what on earth he could have eaten.

Brum in disguise? No. Simon was destined for much greater things. After a few days in the ship's hospital, poor Simon dragged himself back on to deck. His timing was impeccable. His beloved captain had died in the communist attack, and Simon arrived bang on time for his funeral. It is said he sat in silence throughout and turned sadly away when it was all over.

And things were to get worse for Simon. The new captain didn't like him, on account of his being a cat. To add to Simon's problems with the new boss, the overall situation wasn't good aboard his damaged ship. Not daring to rerun the gauntlet of the guns in a dash for the sea, the *Amethyst* was trapped up-river in China and provisions were running low, with an ever growing rodent population destroying what little supplies remained. The gallant and wounded Simon soldiered on, fighting the rats with every ounce of his diminished strength and earning the respect of every sailor aboard. He also spent time in the ship's hospital, visiting and cheering the wounded men. The captain grudgingly had to admit that Simon was handy to have around, but he still wasn't keen. And then, to make matters worse, the captain fell seriously ill. Despite the captain's hostility towards him, Simon kept up a vigil on his bed until he recovered.

While totally agreeing that Simon did a lot for that crew, I wonder about this captain-vigil thing. We all know that cats dive on the laps of the nearest cat-hater. In a row of ten cat-lovers and one hater, they'll always cosy up to the latter. It's what cats do. I have this sneaking suspicion that Simon jumped on the captain's bed and remained there not because he cared in the slightest about his condition, but more because he knew the poor man hated cats and didn't have the strength left in him to object.

The *Amethyst* finally made it to sea, slipping downriver under cover of darkness. And here's a feel-good thing – the thus far feline-detesting captain, so moved and touched by Simon's efforts and enforced companionship during his illness, awarded him a medal and promised to take him in as his own on their return to England.

He was true to his word, regularly visiting Simon in quarantine (ship's cats had to spend six months in quarantine on return to the UK) and looking forward to the day he could collect him. But he never did. Simon grew weak from his wounds during that long wait, and on 28 November 1949 he died.

Simon remains the only cat in history to have received the Dickin Medal for animal valour. He was also the first animal ever to be decorated by the Royal Navy. He was buried with honours, his coffin draped in the Union flag. He lies in the PDSA animal cemetery in Ilford, Essex, and his impressive stone monument reads:

IN MEMORY OF SIMON
SERVED IN HMS AMETHYST
MAY 1948–SEPTEMBER 1949
AWARDED DICKIN MEDAL AUGUST 1949
THROUGHOUT THE YANGTZE INCIDENT HIS
BEHAVIOUR WAS OF THE HIGHEST ORDER.

Very commendable stuff, and about as far removed from Brum as it's possible to get without falling off the edge of the world. 'Unsinkable Sam' was more of a seafaring Brum. Unsinkable Sam was a floating fluffball of bad luck. The fact Sam's first posting was aboard the ill-fated *Bismarck* says it all. The *Bismarck* was duly torpedoed to smithereens, and a desperately catty-paddling Unsinkable was rescued from the sea by the crew of HMS *Cossack*.

With Sam aboard, the *Cossack* sailed on. A few months later, they too were blown out of the water. A fed-up Unsinkable was once more blasted out to sea, only to be dragged half drowned from the water by a sailor aboard HMS *Ark Royal*.

The *Ark Royal*'s crew were now in serious trouble. They had Unsinkable Sam aboard. They never stood a chance. They were pummelled with torpedoes and soon sinking fast. Unsinkable, no doubt believing this sort of thing to be all part of life at sea, swam over to HMS *Legion* and was once again rescued.

By now Sam was famous. And not in a nice way. His new crew knew exactly what they'd pulled out of the water and it was to their immense credit that they didn't throw him back. With the jinx aboard they sailed very carefully back to England and put him ashore. Wherever he ended up living, let's hope it was miles inland and well away from any boating lakes.

Another famous seagoing cat was Mrs Chippy, and Mrs Chippy was another cat Brum could have identified with. Just like Brum, he was dogged with bad luck from the start, and 'he' isn't a misprint. No, Mrs Chippy was a boy. His owner was a carpenter, and so some wag immediately awarded him the position of 'chippy's wife'. How dignified is that? To make matters worse, Mrs Chippy's husband decided it'd be a splendid idea for them to leave the warmth and safety of Britain and head for the coldest and most inhospitable place on Planet Earth. Hence Mrs Chippy and Co. sailed away aboard the *Endurance*, bound for the South Pole.

He turned out to be a popular cat, but not necessarily a bright one. One day, as the ship sailed through the freezing cold Southern Ocean, he suddenly and inexplicably launched himself straight through a porthole. The crew stared aghast as he dropped like a stone into the icy waters below. It took ten minutes to stop the ship and haul him out, by which time he was nearly dead. Not clever behaviour. Not clever at all.

The *Endurance* fared badly. Approaching Antarctica, it became trapped in ice, never to be freed. Hundreds of miles across an empty, frozen sea from anywhere and anything, the crew were stranded, hungry and miserable. Mrs Chippy decided that this would be a smashing time to wind up a pack of vicious and desperately hungry sled-dogs. The resulting mêlée resulted in the pack's handler swinging Mrs Chippy by the scruff of his neck and trying to throw him to the dogs. A caring crew member rescued him, but this cat was most definitely a danger . . . mainly to himself.

While the crew toiled and scrimped to survive, Mrs Chippy slept below decks, actually putting on some weight! But he was a comfort to the crewmen and many believe that his mere presence and total lack of concern for his precarious situation were an inspiration and comfort to the trapped sailors, and so vital to their chances of survival.

I always wonder, when I read about cats in these extraordinary situations, how Brum would have fared. In this case, I don't think he could have done much worse, because Mrs Chippy managed to get himself shot.

The captain, Shackleton, decided that all unnecessary things had to go, and Mrs Chippy was one such thing. It was a terrible shame. Mrs Chippy really wasn't that much of a burden. The men were devastated by the decision, but loyal to Shackleton and so duty bound to carry out his order. One by one the men said there tearful goodbyes, thanking Mrs Chippy for being such a good friend during the long hard voyage together.

Then they gave him a bowl of sardines and shot him. Oh well.

Incidentally, the entire crew made it back alive, owing in most part to the excellent leadership and ingenuity of their captain. But we don't care about them, do we. They shot Mrs Chippy. Stuff 'em. There is, however, an unexpectedly happy ending to all this. After struggling back from the jaws of seemingly certain death, the crew arrived back in England only to be sent off to the First World War and, fittingly, shot. Hah!

I don't really mean it. Then again . . .

Mrs Chippy may have travelled to the worst place on earth, but half a century later another cat managed to get off the earth altogether. Felix, the Astrocat, became the first cat in space in October 1963.

Again, with a piece of dogged Brum-style rotten luck, Felix was plucked from a peaceful existence on the streets of Paris, stuck aboard a high-powered French rocket and blasted over a hundred miles into space. And Felix survived! Separation took place in space and a bemused and wide-eyed Felix drifted back to earth on a parachute. What a cat! A face on numerous worldwide stamps, Felix was, for quite some time, the most famous cat in the world.

But before Felix was even a twinkle in his mother's eye, the seventeenth century's 'Most Famous Feline' award would undoubtedly have fallen to a black cat owned by King Charles I. King Charles did many worthwhile things during his reign, the most notable of which would have to be starting a war that claimed the lives of a quarter of a million of his own subjects, and didn't even involve a foreign enemy.

The English Civil War began in 1642, and King Charles and a certain black cat were two major Royalist figures. The cat became important for strategic reasons. And also rather silly ones. Charles got it into his head that if the cat died, he'd die. Such was his reliance upon the luck exuded by his feline friend, he had him heavily guarded and lavishly waited upon throughout the conflict. The real luck here seems to have all been with the cat, who suddenly became England's most pampered pet.

As the war became bloodier and bloodier and Charles's colleagues, friends and a full one eighth of the English people fell butchered to the floor, you'd think somebody would have noticed that nobody was having an awful lot of luck. But nobody did. The cat got away with it.

There is a strange little twist in this tale. The black cat finally died from natural causes in the latter days of that terrible conflict. The very next day Charles was arrested, and subsequently beheaded. Maybe he was lucky after all, if, that is, the luck revolved around Charles having a head.

A century or so later in France, some more famous royal felines became involved in the French Revolution. Not running around shouting 'Vive la France' and dragging people to the guillotine involved, but involved as the pets of Queen Marie Antoinette. The curious historical distinction of these six long-haired Angoras was that, when a ship arrived to rescue the French queen from the horrors unfolding around her, it was they and not she who boarded and made it to the safety of America. Whether having cats around you is actually a decapitation preventative I don't know, but as Marie Antoinette's half dozen cats sailed happily away to a new life in New England, she herself was having her head cut off.

Despite the dramatic scenario they left behind, the cats are better remembered in American history than they are in French! This isn't because they did anything extraordinary in the New World, but because they did something extremely ordinary – they mated with local cats. In doing so they famously founded the Maine Coon breed, now one of the most popular cats in North America.

I should mention that the above fact is scientifically disputed. But virtually every scientific fact is scientifically disputed, and this theory certainly stands up better to scrutiny than another Maine Coon idea – that the breed originated from the mating of cats and raccoons, hence the name. Despite being a genetic impossibility, the theory still holds sway in certain quarters – probably heavily wooded and remote mountain quarters, but it holds sway nevertheless.

One man who caused more scientific debate than most in his lifetime was the remarkable Sir Isaac Newton, who postulated incredibly-ahead-of-his time theories on mathematics, optics, chemistry and gravity, but most importantly of all invented the cat-flap.

Not many people realise that the cat-flap is responsible for humanity understanding planetary motion, the ebb of tides, the effects of gravity and every other concept Newton explained to us. You see, so irritated was Sir Isaac by the constant miaowing of a pointy-eared furry companion wanting to get in and out of his home that he whipped up a small swinging door to prevent the bewhiskered nuisance further interrupting his train of complicated thought.

I think that, of all the cats I've talked of in this chapter, Brum would have hated being Kitty Newton most of all. Sure, he'd have found being missiled in his bed like poor Simon annoying, and being constantly blown into the cold sea like Unsinkable Sam rather inconvenient. He'd have been positively furious at being shot into space like Felix, and no doubt incensed about being executed like Mrs Chippy.

But an existence as Kitty Newton would have to be his worst nightmare, because Brum has every reason to look back in anger at Sir Isaac Newton. Not only did the man bring the accursed cat-flap into his already problematic life, but Newton also discovered Brum's worst enemy – gravity. Without gravity, Brum could have had a bruise-free life, completely devoid of twenty-foot horror-falls.

Newton has much to answer for.

The Bovine Tiger

'You are what you eat.'

Proverb

Maya had her first exposure to death recently. Sammy had nipped out for a gentle stroll and a breath of fresh air, and so a sparrow lay butchered on the patio. Maya spotted it and legged it back into the house.

'Daddy, Daddy,' she cried. 'A bird's hit its head.'

I agreed that it did indeed look as if it had hit its head. Quite badly.

Maya suggested that it might have fallen out of a tree and asked when it would wake up. I told her it'd be OK soon and ushered her back inside, mentioning that *Bob the Builder* had just started as I know this simple daily event ends all rational thought.

I fully intended to go and dispose of the body but . . . you know, I got into *Bob the Builder* and all rational thought left my head too. I stared, totally enthralled, as Bob tried to convince some poor old lady that her roof needed fixing when it didn't

and then kicked over her garden wall and offered to fix it for five hundred quid. Something like that anyway. About three hours later I was just getting into *Dora the Explorer* when Maya came back into the room (I've no idea how long she'd been gone) with a thoughtful, worried expression on her face.

She sat down next to me, clearly thinking very hard indeed, something quite disturbingly alien in our house. I finally gave in, accepted that I'd now never know whether Dora managed to recapture Boots the Monkey's red welly, and asked what was troubling her. She led me by the hand to the back door and stared out at the bird, which was still dead.

I winced and silently cursed Bob and all of his kind.

'Daddy?'

'Yes, Maya?' I replied, a little too defensively.

'Bird's not good . . .'

Bird's not good. Understating the problem possibly but I couldn't have put it better myself. I felt I needed to come clean and clarify things.

'Well, Maya, um, yes, you see, er, these things, they, er, happen, and they happen to . . . birds. OK? Understand? Good!'

I could see from her perplexed face that this wasn't OK and she didn't understand. I tried again.

'Well, Maya, the thing is, it's like this, you see, the bird didn't just hurt its head. Sammy got it and . . . I'm afraid it won't get much better.'

'Oh?'

'Yes, sometimes Sammy can be very bad for birds.'

'Bird won't get better?'

'No, it won't.'

'Oh . . . it dead, then, is it?'

At least she was showing some degree of concern for the bird. When I was her age, a similar drama unfolded. A badly injured bird was sitting in the garden, having got into a nasty fight with Ringo Starr (a local tabby – cats have always been utter bastards really, haven't they?). Dad knelt down and solemnly asked me how we could help the poor little thing. 'Hit it on the head with a shovel, Daddy,' came my happy reply.

There's a photo of me as a three-year-old wearing a coat three sizes too big and pointing at a gravestone, seemingly in fits of laughter. I must have been a very strange kid indeed.

The day after the bird's unfortunate demise (cold-blooded slaughter), Maya watched a wildlife documentary about big cats. They were bigger, and in some cases stripier, but they were a lot like Sammy. Suddenly Maya got it; everything clicked into place. All cats kill things. It's their job, just like Mummy's is driving off in the car and doing 'stuff' and Daddy's is . . . not sure Daddy does anything, but pretty sure it's something to do with gazebos that he doesn't do. And there was more. The bigger the cat, the bigger the killed things. Sammy caught that bird but her chances of dragging home a zebra were slim. Lions and tigers were evidently even tougher than Sammy, and in any case, Sammy had got a bit too smiley of late. This instantly made them the coolest thing in Maya's life.

Not that I necessarily agreed with Maya's views. I think that if a domestic cat were the size of a lion or tiger, it would be a far more dangerous proposition than either. Why? Because the domestic cat is a murderous psychopath, that's why!

There's a whole world of domestic cats out there, just itching to kill for fun. I've often marvelled at this strange preoccupation with murder. Murder may sound a bit strong, but think about it: cats, in many countries at least, are well fed and watered. They have no need to kill, but they *like* to. They set out to kill, not for food, not for survival, but as a hobby. No other animal, besides humans, has a hobby like that.

Sure, some animals can go off the rails into a mad blood frenzy at times (I know I can), but cats kill with a happy smile and a seeming sense of utter joy. Look at how Sammy's ill-fated bird must have copped it – 'La-de-da-de-da – ah, the sunshine, the scent of flowers, what a lovely summer's day . . . hang on, I'll just murder this sparrow . . . it makes you happy to be alive, tra-la-la.' Bloody little maniacs.

But Maya's opinions are her own, and her obsession with lions and tigers became so great that she'd spend hours crawling on all fours roaring at people (and startled cats) and playfully gouging at their eyes with claw-like fingers. We decided to take her to the zoo to see the real thing, hoping she wouldn't pick up a tip or two on mauling.

We were as excited as she was, and I haven't been excited about zoos since a 1976 school trip to Whipsnade, when a free-range wallaby stole my duffel bag. A quarter of an hour it took me to get it back, running back and forth across a muddy field in front of all my jeering classmates. And I only got it then because the stupid little bouncing marsupial git dropped it in a pile of crap. Anyway, no need to get all bitter and twisted about wallabies again. That was a long time ago. Move on. Let it go.

We went through the elephants and giraffes at breakneck speed. All Maya wanted to see was a lion. We came to a picnic green and I pointed, misguidedly, to the lion enclosure on its far side. Maya was off, bounding full throttle across the green, straight over tartan picnic rugs, closely followed by me and then, some way back, Lorraine, who may be good at many things but her dash and reaction are less than brilliant – putting one very much in mind of the *QE2* on a two-mile turning manoeuvre.

By the time I caught Maya mid-stride and lifted her wildly kicking body over the centre of a disgruntled family's lunch, she was totally breathless and constantly repeating the line 'Huh huh huh cough lions lions LIONS'. It was like a scene from a Tarzan movie.

We waited for a very long time, and when Lorraine finally arrived, constantly repeating the line 'Huh huh huh cough Maya Maya MAYA', we walked the final ten yards and joined a huge throng around the lion cage. A lioness stood atop a boulder, head held high as if posing for a photo shoot, aloof and proud.

Maya stared at her for some time. Finally she muttered, 'Cow.'

Cow? Cow? Did she think this magnificent creature was a cow?

Lorraine and I looked at one another and then at Maya and both repeated, 'Cow?'

'Cow,' confirmed Maya. She turned and left.

We hurried after her, trying to explain she'd just seen an agile, streamlined killing machine, not a cumbersome grass-muncher, but she was having none of it. She wanted to see a tiger now. That had to be impressive. Surely.

It was. Tigers are top cats. Tigers are even tougher than lions. And stripier. And this tiger was furious. Zoos are often classed as cruel and, watching this poor animal working itself into a frenzy of rage at the crowd of people leering at it, you had to agree.

But the tiger did look incredibly mean and impressive, just two feet away on the other side of a reinforced sheet of glass so unnervingly clear that it appeared not to be there at all. When the livid beast suddenly lurched at us and growled, everybody instinctively jumped backwards. Not Maya, though. She jumped forward. In fact, she pounced.

The slightly surprised tiger glared at this impudent cub and gave an ear-splitting roar. Maya, nose to nose with an enraged tiger, stared back in a bored sort of way and whispered, 'Moo.'

Then she turned on her heels, spat the word 'cow' with utter contempt and paced off to find some monkeys. The tiger watched her go. His fearsome symmetry had been compromised – he had failed to even slightly bother a pint-sized Mowgli in a dress. In his face I could see the type of disappointment Brum experiences on a daily basis.

Maya's big-cat admiration was over – very quickly replaced by an obsession with a leering chimpanzee and a penchant for asking very awkward questions along the lines of 'What was the funny thing the big monkey was doing in its prison?' Nasty, vile little creature. The chimp, that is, not Maya.

I've pondered Maya's big-cat attitude since, and I must assume that, despite all I've said about the sheer murderousness of the average domestic feline, living with Brum all her life has so thoroughly eroded her ability to take cats seriously that she fails to see even a snarling tiger as anything more deadly than a cow.

Dave's Diary

'Ignorance of one's misfortunes is clear gain.'

Euripides

Poppy, our next-door-neighbour cat, has long been attached to a piece of string. As she's slightly loopy and prone to wandering merrily into oncoming traffic, her owner has restricted her outdoor activities by keeping her on a long length of string, attached to a heavy weight at the top of his steps.

In the year and a half since Poppy moved in next door, Brum's fascination with her, or more likely her bit of string, hasn't waned. He never dares go too close, instead watching awestruck from a distance, usually from our front wall. Sammy can't be bothered with it all. She behaves as if Poppy and her bit of string aren't even there. I'm sure her attitude would be something along the lines of 'Yeah, like, soooo? . . . it's a bit of string, Brum, get over it'. Having said that, I now wonder whether her falling off the wall wasn't caused by leaning too far out for a sneaky voyeuristic string-peek. You never know.

Sammy may or may not be interested in string or Poppy, but she does get much closer to both of them than Brum. Sammy uses the rooftops as a mode of transport, something Brum rarely does, thankfully. As our house is joined to Poppy's, Sammy will often stroll over Poppy's head and suddenly plop down beside her, giving the poor befuddled cat a near-heart-attack before casually carrying on her way, making no attempt at friendly small talk whatsoever.

I strongly suspect Brum watched Sammy do this on more than one occasion before deciding to try it out for himself. The possibility of Brum 'dropping in unexpectedly' and not landing with a force normally associated with a thousand-megaton bomb is almost non-existent. Something had to go badly wrong. It did.

On a roof full of tiny tiles, one was bound to be loose. The

chances
of Brum
finding that particular
tile were evens at best. My
neighbour, Dave, just happened
to be out in his front garden when events
unfolded. How terrible if he hadn't been. How
terrible it would have been if nobody had witnessed
this act of tragicomic genius. How many of Brum's
classic stunts *are* missed?

The moment Dave saw Brum on the roof he clasped
his hands to his head and gritted his teeth. What on earth
was that bloody cat going to do this time?

Whereas Sammy skips daintily along the sloping rooftops, I'm
reliably informed that Brum executed the manoeuvre in exactly
the same way you'd expect a horse to. He was all over the place.
His legs kept splaying out in opposite directions. He was moving
sideways, one paw at a time, his face set in tense concentration.
As he reached a point somewhere above Poppy's head, he began
a slow, anxious descent towards the guttering.

All the while, he was emitting a high-pitched miaowing sound
(I've no idea why) and this somehow slowly penetrated Poppy's
dulled senses (we really are dealing with two 'switched-on' cats
here, aren't we).

She began looking around, trying to work out where the cat
noises were coming from. Finally she looked up.

She could see nothing because of the overhang, so decided to
jump on to the wall in front of the house to take a look (Dave's
front wall is exactly the same as ours, by the way – a flight of
steps leads up to a walled path that runs along the front of the
house to the front door. In front of the wall is a steep drop to
the lawn).

At the precise moment Poppy jumped, Brum hit the loose tile,
his careful descent became a full-on galloping run and he leapt
from the roof at a 45-degree angle. He missed Poppy by a cat's
whisker, sailing past her over the wall and immediately plunging

down towards Dave on the lawn below.

Suddenly, a stunned Poppy was wrenched sideways by the neck and came careering down with him. Brum had missed her, but not her bit of string, which had stretched out on the wall alongside her, providing a sudden obstacle for Brum, who hurtled into it and took it with him like a feline marathon winner. In all the excitement Dave stepped back into a bush, lost his footing and fell out on to the pavement, just as two cats crashed at his upturned feet with piercing shrieks.

From the wall swung Poppy's vacated elastic collar.

Dave retrieved Poppy, and Brum made his own way home. No sooner had Dave safely deposited the shocked and shaken Poppy back through his door than he was excitedly knocking on mine.

Brum had only just joined me as I opened the door to find a bedraggled neighbour in fits of helpless laughter. He couldn't even speak, he just pointed at Brum and started laughing even louder.

Brum stared at me with wide-eyed wonder and I stared at Brum. At that moment I seriously considered the possibility that the man next door was a madman. How often does somebody come knocking at your door merely to laugh at your cat? I stood for a while, waiting for him to calm down, but he couldn't. It became infectious. I started laughing. I swear Brum was laughing too, but I couldn't hear a thing over our guffaws – he may well have been hissing.

At this point, he gripped my arm and just walked off.

I watched him go, coughing and spluttering between his laughs as he disappeared through his front door.

I went inside, where Lorraine was skilfully juggling Maya and a cup of tea.

'What were you two finding so hilarious?' asked Lorraine.

'I have absolutely no idea,' I told her, honestly.

When Dave finally felt well enough to speak again, he told me the full, sorry tale. He said that he knew there was going to be an accident the moment he saw Brum up there. What other cat can instil that sort of confidence, or complete lack of it? A cat on a roof should be an 'easy viewing' sort of sight. They do it all the time. Why would you think they'd fall? It was at this point that Dave began reeling off a catalogue of accidents that, until that point, I'd no idea Brum had been involved in. My niggling suspicion that I miss many of Brum's crazy antics suddenly became solid fact.

I knew that Brum was a curse to delivery people, for instance; mainly the paper boy, and he'd certainly worried the postman. I had no idea, though, that our local milkman hated him. Our milkman *hates* Brum. At a time of the morning when even Maya isn't usually awake, and an hour Lorraine and I hadn't even seen until Maya occasionally insisted we take a look, Brum is out there actively falling out with milkmen.

'Why does the milkman hate him?' I asked, astonished.

'I don't know,' replied Dave, 'he just keeps saying he hates him. Gets quite upset about it.'

Amazing.

And what's more, Brum has been rescued from a near-drowning in Dave's water butt.

In desperately familiar fashion on a bitterly cold February day, ʾhim out by the scruff leaping gazelle-like over Dave's fence and him down, all the time receiving viciously grateful lacerations.

All this went on without my having an inkling!

A neighbour saves Brum's life, by sheer chance happening to

84

come out of his door at the moment he plops into a water butt, and I don't find out until five months later. Dave deserved a medal, but he 'didn't think it worth mentioning!'

A bit worrying that Brum's biting the neighbours, though. I know he'd bite one only if under considerable provocation and, to Brum, being hauled back from the jaws of death is 'considerable provocation', but I try to get on with my neighbours and make it the Golden Rule never to bite them (something I've generally been able to stick to).

Being careful not to gnaw on his arm, I eagerly asked Dave whether he'd ever seen Brum catch fire, this being something he used to be so good at. Sadly he hadn't and seemed surprised at the question, which was odd because he'd seen plenty of things that should have made the notion of a combustible tabby perfectly acceptable.

Among the most amazing of those things, according to my new Brum-incident-oracle, was the day he saw Brum outwitted by a squirrel. Now, this in itself didn't come as surprising news. Most creatures tend to get the better of him in some way or other, and in any battle of wits Brum is always going to be unarmed. But the next few revelations did surprise me somewhat.

Sammy had been on the scene, and had also been totally duped by this cunning tree-rat. Also, Brum and Sammy appeared to have been hunting the squirrel, together, when the incident occurred. Brum hunting? Brum and Sammy working together to bring down a squirrel? Unbelievable. There had to be a mistake.

Sammy made all the initial moves, stalking the squirrel as Dave watched from his kitchen window. She came within one short pounce of success before Dave banged on his window, alerting the imperilled squirrel to the nightmare about to land on its back.

The shocked squirrel darted towards a clump of trees, just as a familiar tabby face emerged from them.

It was here that I had to disagree with Dave's suggestion that Brum and Sammy were on a joint mission. I'm pretty certain that at this point Brum would have been just as surprised as the squirrel, but it certainly must have looked every bit like an orchestrated attack. Certainly to the squirrel, who reacted first and was well away before Brum even moved a muscle (that's more like it), running straight at Sammy and then, just as Sammy thought she had a second chance, launching into the air and landing halfway up the only tree in the middle of Dave's lawn.

It's more of an ex-tree really – a long, thin trunk, rising straight up to ten feet in height with no branches whatsoever. The squirrel climbed to the top, but now he was totally trapped. His tree trunk was well out of jump-range to any nearby bushes or proper trees, and all that surrounded him was open lawn and two stalking cats. Or rather, one stalking cat and one who probably had no idea what he was doing there.

The cats sat and watched in that intimidating way of theirs, that mock uninterested coolness (in Brum's case – genuine blank-ness). The squirrel weighed up his options. All looked hopeless. But then he did an unexpectedly clever thing. He began climbing down the trunk, straight towards his tormentors.

Both cats, even Brum, closed in on him. As he got lower, they got closer, moving in for the kill. As he descended to just four feet, the cats reached the trunk. At this point he leapt clean over their heads and scampered into the clump of trees. Brilliant! He'd lured them in, pulled them together, got them close enough to jump over, and leapfrogged them.

Dave was so impressed he cheered. Sammy looked livid and Brum looked at Sammy. A livid Sammy isn't nice. The last Dave saw of them was the rear end of Brum being hotly pursued by Sammy, who no doubt felt he'd be easier quarry than any squirrel.

Had he seen anything else? I pressed him. He seemed perplexed now. His next-door neighbour wanted to talk about cats all day. He was even more perplexed when I whipped out a notebook. Trying to ignore my mad-eyed eagerness, he bravely pressed on.

'W-w-well,' he stammered, 'there's been quite a few little things really. You don't want to hear about any more of them . . . do you?'

I almost bit him, but instead nodded violently.

'Er, OK, OK,' he said, backing away slightly. 'Let's see . . . I know. This is brilliant actually. It was one of those red kites from over the fields.'

'RED KITES, RED KITES! BRILLIANT, YES!'

He started chortling as he recalled the memory: 'It was circling over the houses. It must have seen something on the ground, prey or something, because it got lower and lower and ended up circling my garden. I was watching it, as you do, and then I noticed Brum on the top lawn [Dave has two lawn layers, separated by a wall that finishes flush with the top lawn, just like ours]. Brum was staring up at it. He seemed totally fascinated, really concentrating on what it was doing.

'Then he started mimicking its flight pattern, walking round and round the lawn in great big circles. The kite started climbing back higher, but still circling, and the circles got bigger and bigger. Brum's circles got bigger too. He looked totally ridiculous, his head was pointing straight up in the air and he kept walking round and round the garden, his circles getting bigger all the time. If you hadn't seen the kite, you'd have thought he'd gone crazy. The kite kept circling, Brum kept circling, the kite's circles got bigger still, Brum's circles got bigger still. I could see it coming. He wasn't looking where he was going at all, what with staring straight up in the sky. His last circuit was far too big. He just walked clean off the wall. Clean off it. Just waltzed straight over the edge.

He looked completely stunned. He dropped seven feet, legs still trying to walk, hit the ground and went into a defensive crouch – it was like 'Where am I? How did I get here?' I was creased up. And then, all sort of befuddled, he tried to jump back on the wall, but he was way off target – he went straight up like a rocket, his head cracked the wall overhang and his whole body

87

scrunched up and flipped over, so his backside shot higher than his head and he collapsed back to the ground in a heap . . . I don't know where the kite had gone . . . I've got to go now . . . OK?'

I let him go. He'd had enough.

A couple of weeks later I asked the milkman why he hated my cat. He looked a little taken aback. It's not the sort of question you expect someone to ask you. I explained I was writing a book, and he relaxed slightly – but only slightly, because I think something in the mention of Brum annoyed him.

Silently, he rolled up his standard-issue Express Dairies trouser leg. He did it in a way that reminded me of a man pulling up his sleeves for a fight. For a moment I thought he was about to start kicking me. But then he pointed to some seriously nasty scarring around his knee. I stared, aghast. What was he showing me here? Had Brum savaged this man?

He rolled his trouser leg back down and started back towards his float.

'Did my cat do that?' I called out, aghast.

He stopped dead.

Turning around, he regarded me, a little reproachfully, and walked back over.

'No, of course not. He's only a cat, not a ruddy tiger!' he said, and then started laughing aloud. We both laughed together, me with a frown of confusion. Suddenly he stopped laughing and added, 'No, he didn't do it. It was his bloody fault, though. Little pest runs at me every day, comes bounding down them steps like a ruddy torpedo. Hits my legs hard, he does. Heavy little sod too.'

Why? I asked myself, not wanting to interrupt. He doesn't bowl himself at other visitors' legs.

As if answering my silent question, the milkman continued:

'I reckon it's the milk that excites him. Anyway, back in the winter he came at me one morning and your steps were icy; he lost his footing, hit me sideways, I slipped, dropped two pints of milk and fell on 'em. I lay there with blood gushing down my legs while that flaming cat purred like a train and lapped up the milk.'

The poor bloke! All this and he never thought to mention it, not even in a solicitor's letter. What is it with these people? If my cat puts someone in hospital, then I want to know about it.

'Look, I'm really sorry . . .' I started to say, but the milkman stopped me with a wave of an arm and a shrug.

He walked back to his float, before turning and adding, 'I saw your missus in town the other day. You sorted that gazebo out yet?'

With that final shot to my heart, he sped off down the road at 5 mph.

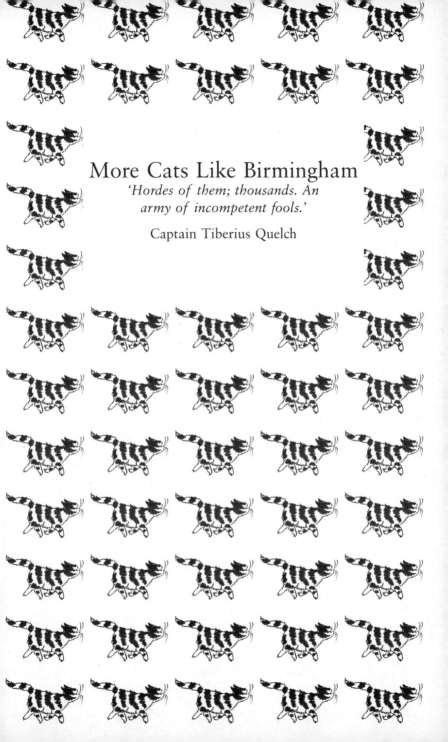

More Cats Like Birmingham

'Hordes of them; thousands. An army of incompetent fools.'

Captain Tiberius Quelch

The release of my first book, *A Cat Called Birmingham*, brought forth a deluge of fan mail. Well . . . not a deluge exactly. I got a few letters. And not all exactly 'fan' letters – a letter from Slough opened with the line YOU TOSSER. The same letter went on to say, 'There's absolutely nothing wrong with Slough. It's the people who live here. THEY'RE ALL TOSSERS LIKE YOU.' By the end of the letter I became confused as to who exactly the sender was annoyed with. The last line was even more confusing: 'More of the same please!' More of the same? My first effort was enough to infuriate and induce impassioned hated, and yet she wanted more. If nothing else, the letter made me realise I have more in common with the people of Slough than I'd previously thought – and not because we're all tossers, more because the Slough sender was a complete lunatic. I couldn't help but like her.

Quite a few of the letters, however, were very interesting and very funny. Lots of people told me all about their own cats, likening them to Brum. Receiving these was therapeutically rewarding – words of comfort from fellow sufferers.

And most comforting of all was Lisa from Essex. Lisa has three cats, and two of them are normal. Then there's Alfred, who is mad. Not in the conventional 'cat' way either. No, Alfred thinks he's Napoleon Bonaparte. This cat's conviction that he's the former Emperor of France isn't so much a problem as an oddity. In fact Alfred has become something of a celebrity, even appearing in his local newspaper. For hours a day, he will sit atop his front gatepost, his body raised like that of a gopher so that only his rear end is seated. One front paw hangs limply by his side, while the other rests imperiously across his chest. Lisa sent me a photo of his peculiar posturing, and he really does look remarkably like

Napoleon. As Alfred grandly surveys all from his gatepost throne, crowds of children gather in the street to stare back, enthralled. Passing motorists often swerve dangerously upon sighting this odd feline apparition. One day, for fun, Lisa placed a homemade tricorn hat upon Alfred's head. He seemed to like it, and it was this picture which made the papers, with the reporter cleverly noting that when Alfred adopts his peculiar stance, he stares longingly towards the nearby sea . . . and in the general direction of France. No doubt in my mind – he's Napoleon alright.

Debbie from Birmingham wrote to correct me on a particular issue. It would appear that Brum isn't the only cat capable of being knocked senseless. Her cat Trigger achieved that very feat, and in much the same way a boxer would. Debbie has two young daughters, aged three and five. The pair are a formidable combination. The three-year-old goads, annoys and ultimately starts fights, the five-year-old finishes them.

Poor old Trigger finally snapped one day and, fed up with being poked, prodded and pinched by his three-year-old friend, launched himself full length at her, flying in for the kill. But little Miss Five-year-old Bruiser was too quick for him, protecting her sister with a full-blown left-hook haymaker that caught Trigger mid-flight and sent him crashing to the canvas. One – two – three – OUT! Trigger lay twitching on the ground in cloud-cuckoo-land. Knocked out by a toddler's blow to the jaw! He came round and was soon as right as rain, but wow, that poor cat. Now while I'd like to make it clear that I disagree in principle with punching your cat, I do think it's sometimes fun. No, hang on, not fun . . . necessary – I meant to say necessary (in Brum's case, very much so). The consequences of Trigger's claws connecting with little Miss Irritating's face could have been nasty in the extreme, so best to knock Trigger for six before he got there. I doubt Trigger would agree.

If the madness of emperor-cat Alfred is comforting to me, then Trigger's misfortune must be doubly reassuring for Brum. Not only has Brum never been downed with a punch, but it would appear he's got it relatively easy with Maya. But then she's not five yet, is she?

Mark from Birmingham read one particular story from my

first book with a deepening frown. It was too close to an experience of his own. The original story concerned a cat who switched off a modem and shut down a hundred courier companies. Mark's cat Spock (named for his black shiny fur and pointed ears!) didn't do anything quite so elaborate, but on a personal level it was every bit as terrible.

Mark had been on the end of a serious telephone rollicking from his boss. After much subsequent deliberation he decided that he couldn't stomach the complaints thrown at him and needed to tell the lady concerned exactly what he thought of her. It was a major, life-changing decision. His job was a well-paid one that he had been very happy in. But his need to retaliate outweighed rational common sense, and he felt he couldn't carry on in his role in the light of what had been said. With a heavy heart he switched on his computer and wrote an emotive e-mail resignation. Not a pleasant 'After many happy years it is with great regret'-type resignation, you understand. More an 'I've always hated you, you ****ing vindictive bitch' affair. When the e-mail was complete he read and re-read it, adding the odd four-letter pleasantry here and there but never changing its tone. Halfway through his fourth reading, the phone rang. He left the room to answer the call, which turned out to be from his boss. She'd been thinking about their conversation too, and felt she'd been rather unfair on Mark and so had called to offer her sincerest apologies. Mark accepted and the pair talked optimistically about a long and happy future together.

Mark punched the air in delight upon replacing the receiver and strode back to his computer to delete his offensive e-mail. What if that phone had rung five minutes later, he thought, what if I'd sent that awful, vile, insulting piece of trash before my boss had called to apologise? Phew, that was a close one. He walked back into his study . . .

Spock had sent the e-mail.

The cat who'd just cost Mark his lucrative job lay sprawled across his desk, purring contentedly, his chin resting on the keyboard. Emblazoned across the glowing screen were the horrific, jaw-dropping words 'YOUR E-MAIL HAS BEEN SENT'.

Apparently, they were round to collect his company car and mobile phone within the hour. To add insult to injury, Spock brushed happily around the two burly company security men's legs with loving affection. I wonder whether Spock can ever have needed beaming up more than he did that day.

Very interestingly, a lady from South Africa wrote to say she'd once been in possession of a 'Feline Evolution Toilet Seat' (the American-manufactured 'attach to your WC seat' for cats). Alas, she never used it . . . well, she wouldn't use it, of course . . . the cat would normally use it. She left it on a train on her way home from the shops. The funniest thing was her attempt to explain to the lost property department exactly what it was she'd lost:

'A toilet seat, madam?'

'Yes. A cat's toilet seat.'

'Cats have toilets?'

'No. Just toilet seats.'

'But not toilets?'

'No.'

'What exactly do they do with these seats, then, madam?'

The seat was never recovered. Some cat, somewhere, would have been sitting smugly on the loo, reading *Cat World* and whistling happily, while another poor cat (the 'almost owner' of an expensive Feline Evolution Toilet Seat) still had to scramble around in urine-soaked clay trying to bury its own faeces. A cat's life can be very unfair.

On a toilet-related theme, Laura from Dorset wrote to tell me about curiously unfeline goings-on in her native seaside town. As the town is a fishing port, the harbour front tends to attract a large number of cats. Every morning the furry entourage congregates around the incoming boats and feasts on fresh off-cuts and scraps. On the harbourside is a public convenience. During the course of the morning, possibly as a direct result of the subliminal effects of being so close to so much swirling water and breaking waves, one or two cats will be caught short. When they need to go, unbelievably they use the public lavatories. One by one, a tabby or a marmalade, a tortoiseshell or a Siamese, will trudge off to the Gents, relieve themselves at the urinals and head back to resume their quayside vigil!

WHAT! Cats using a public toilet? Nonsense, surely. Cats would never, ever adhere to such institutionalised behaviour. Would they? Laura maintains they do.

Her theory is that the urinals have become contested territory, and the cats are scenting the area. She has video footage of it happening! What a peculiar sight. Imagine standing at a urinal (sorry if you're not a bloke and quite rightly don't want to imagine that), when suddenly a couple of cats troop in, stand either side of you, take a leak, sigh, shake their tails and slink back out again.

I think you'd seriously consider the possibility that something in the urinal's cleaning chemicals had caused a temporary imbalance in your mind!

It's funny I should have received letters of this nature. Public toilets have become quite a feature of my own life nowadays. That's quite a disturbing admission, isn't it? But it's true. It has a lot to do with Maya. You see, accompanying Maya into a public lavatory can be a bit of a trial. We tend to congratulate her for her ablutions at home – encouragement for using the potty or toilet and not her pants. She now knows the system and feels that it's a thing worth celebrating. And so, after I'd plonked her on the toilet in a supermarket Gents and applauded her accordingly, she felt the need to return the compliment come my turn.

Consequently, as I stood there in the cubicle, a toddler suddenly danced a jig of undiluted joy behind me, and began screaming at the top of her voice, 'YOU'RE WEEING, DADDY, YOU'RE WEEING, WELL DONE, WELL DONE, YOU'RE WEEING IN THE TOILET NOW, YOU CLEVER BOY!'

As I washed my hands, two old chaps alongside me looked ready to laugh aloud. I smiled resignedly. As they left the room one of them glanced back at me, nodded sincerely and said, 'Well done, lad . . . well done.'

All of which, however, is far, far better than not making it to the toilet at all. A friend of mine will attest to that. When he was browsing in the outdoor gardening section of a local DIY store, his two-year-old son suddenly attacked him with the panic-inducing words, 'Daddy! Toilet! Now! I doing it now!'

Knowing there to be no in-store public toilets, he went into silly mode. His son was about to wet his pants and so, as a responsible parent, he decided he had the right to take whatever action necessary – however stupid.

He glanced around the deserted arena of bedding plants and patio ornaments, satisfied himself that nobody was near by, grabbed a terracotta plant pot, whipped his boy's trousers down and plonked him on it.

'In the pot, Daddy?'

'In the pot, son.'

A quick wee in a pot, he thought. Nobody would moan about that, surely. Then a horrible, horrible thought struck him.

'This is a wee you're doing . . . is it?'

'Poo, Daddy.'

So . . . there he was, standing in a shop, with his son excreting in a plant pot. He had to do something quick, so he performed a little-known Native American dance that involved hopping from foot to foot, chanting, 'Ooo, no, ooo, no,' and circling a toddler on a terracotta planter.

No sooner had his lad happily announced that he was done than he was airborne, being wrenched from his makeshift potty and retrousered in a split second. My friend stared at the pot in dismay. How could a tiny toddler have done a thing like that? It was huge – a gigantic steaming turd, something you'd have expected more from a lumberjack than a two-year-old boy.

No choice but to go and fetch the manager . . . he thought as he grabbed his son and legged it out of the shop without a word. Nightmare flashes of an unsuspecting customer grabbing the pot and checking its price with a quick and terrible flip long assailed his troubled mind.

His wife still remembers exactly where she was when he phoned her to tell her what he'd done. She says she always will.

Anyway, I received one further letter on the subject of ablutions. A reader named Pia informed me of her cat Whisky's habit of jumping into her empty bath and relieving himself down the plughole.

The reader seemed to be very happy about this. As she'd enclosed her e-mail address, I wrote and asked why. 'Better than on the carpet,' she replied. Doesn't your bathroom stink of cat urine, I asked. 'Not at all, he's an excellent shot!'

Two months after we agreed to disagree on the merits of your cat urinating in your bath, Brum urinated in the bath. He hopped in as I stood cleaning my teeth, raised his head and tail, closed his eyes in blissful contentment and sent a jet straight down the plughole. I watched in stunned silence. Had he read Pia's e-mail? Where had he got this idea from? Perhaps he'd been doing it for years – I have no idea, but he was certainly doing it now! To say that Brum is also an excellent shot doesn't do the boy justice. His stream was so spot-on that it splashed and tinkled into the plughole without touching the sides. And it went on for ages. Much too long. I tapped my foot and waited for him to finish for nearly a minute. It was like watching an elephant go. When he'd finally finished, he simply hopped out of the bath with an air of total nonchalance.

'Oi!' I shouted. 'You wait just one moment, Birmingham. You're in big trouble!'

But he didn't think so. He seemed very pleased with himself indeed. And I'm not exactly sure whether he should or shouldn't have been. I inspected the bath after he'd gone. Not a drip seemed to have missed its target. Now, when I think about it, isn't this the perfect place for a cat to pee? If you turn the tap on regularly, isn't it the same as a toilet flush? Isn't this a far better option than a smelly, unhygienic litter tray? I think it probably is, and I e-mailed Pia to tell her so. 'But doesn't Brum have a cat-flap and a garden to go to the toilet in?' she e-mailed back. 'Yes,' I replied.

'Well – that's disgusting, then,' she said.

Brilliant. We'd gone full circle. Whisky lives at the top of a high-rise and uses his brains. Brum's a lazy and disgusting slob. Settled.

One reader-letter in particular came as a big surprise. It was from a lady named Natalie, who told me all about a troublesome cat she'd owned in the sixties. What was really amazing about the letter was the address at the top. I couldn't quite believe it. Natalie lived two doors down from Peanuts.

Peanuts had a whole chapter of *A Cat Called Birmingham* devoted to him. Peanuts was a double-hard mad-psycho cat, who scared the life out of Brum and serial-killed rabbits, leaving only one paw and a bobtail as evidence of each grisly slaughter. And Natalie was his neighbour. Isn't it a strange world? She read all about a psychotic cat in a book, without realising it was the cat next door but one!

That letter brought back memories! Natalie still lives in the road, but Peanuts moved away a few years ago. I decided to track him down. Not through a newspaper column or anything – PEANUTS. WE ARE MISSING YOU. PLEASE CONTACT US. WE LOVE YOU – but through his owners, a couple named Heather and Simon.

Through various old e-mail addresses, etc., I found him. He now lives in the French Alps! Heather's description of Peanuts as an old man of the mountains was so funny that I feel it's my duty to print it here:

Peanuts is well. He still has one tooth left and is now very deaf . . . which can prove exciting for him at times. He's so deaf that we try to throw shadows across him as we approach by way of compensating for his lack of hearing – otherwise things get a bit chaotic. Unfortunately the cats that he spent the whole of last year beating to a pulp aren't quite so considerate, so he's learnt to sit with his back against the wall. We don't have rabbits here – all the snakes/eagles and other wild animals have eaten them – so Peanuts chases lizards now, but with just one tooth left – Peanuts, not the lizards – it proves quite interesting and he tells me they are extremely bitter. Well, who wouldn't be while being gummed to death? He has also learnt to speak French and now meows loudly, with such a tone of distress and misery, and continues this verbal onslaught for such prolonged periods of time, that we find ourselves wondering if he has been possessed or if he's auditioning for *The X Factor*. I read some of your book out to Peanuts, including the bit about him being the

'Australian cure-all' (for ridding Australia of their epidemic of rabbits), which he seemed rather pleased by, but while I found it highly amusing he seemed to take it all rather seriously as though it were a distinct possibility.

A distinct possibility indeed. The scourge of rabbits! I've yet to meet a bigger worry to the leporine world than that lad.

Finally, a letter from Violet from County Antrim.

I've learnt all about her hot-water-bottle-hugging cat of bygone times. This cat had an old stone pot variety of water bottle to snuggle up to, but of course hot-water bottles nowadays are a much flimsier proposition. A modern rubber-bottle-hugging Brum could have you waking in the dead of night convinced you'd had a very nasty accident indeed.

Violet is catless these days, and has long considered taking in another feline friend, but worries that the possibility of ending up with a 'Brum' is too risky. I have to admit that, judging by the letters I've received, the chances of another Brum are higher than previously thought. But so what – a Brum's better than no cat at all, even if there *is* every chance it will totally destroy your house, self-confidence and life.

Go on, Violet – get another cat.

Beggar, Billy, Barmy Spy

*'How is it that little children are so intelligent
and men so stupid? It must be education
that does it.'*

Alexandre Dumas

ometimes I like to be independent. Sometimes I like to shrug off Maya and Brum and make a complete idiot of myself without assistance. Striking a blow for the free idiot.

To help me along with my stupid plans, I work part time in a call centre as a market researcher. For those of you who think market research is an easy, non-dangerous job – think again. I know the only apparent dangers of a job involving talking and key-tapping would be falling off your chair or smacking yourself in the eye with a phone, but not only is research dangerous, it can be cool, suave and debonair. You see, as a market researcher with a prestigious double-0[*] prefix, I am sometimes sent 'into the field' on spying missions. The intelligence branch of market research is known as mystery shopping and I, Chris Pascoe, am a man of mystery . . . a Mystery Shopper.

In the interests of market research, and maybe national security but probably not, I visit restaurants, pubs and cinemas and pretend to be someone else. I then have to slip off into the toilets to update top-secret dossiers on all staff I've interacted with, and also to check there's adequate toilet paper. It's a sneaky sort of job, but it's great. I'm employed to watch movies, eat food and drink beer. That's more or less all I ever do anyway, and these people pay me for it.

As my job involves doing . . . well, nothing, my superiors believe I'm capable of little more than nothing and treat me like a moron. Either it's the job or they just happen to have met me and know very well that I'm a moron.

Either way, I regularly receive mission memos of the following

[*]Zero productivity, zero success rate.

nature, which in most cases seem to have been written by some-body equally as bright as I'm considered to be:

Reference Pizza Restaurant Visit: With regard to note 5 (checking the pizza is at an acceptable temperature upon reaching your table) we would stress that you must on no account use a thermometer. Repeat, DO NOT USE A THERMOMETER. This may arouse the suspicions of restaurant staff.

Reference Name Badges: As you know, it is imperative that you record the name of all members of staff you deal with. Their name can be located on their name badge. Please do not write staff members' names down in their presence, as this may cause concern. Please note that staff are required to wear their name badges at all times, and it is therefore important that you record the names of any members of staff not wearing a name badge [how??]. It should also be noted that the manager of an establishment is not required to wear a uniform or name badge. The manager can be identified as he will not be wearing a uniform or name badge.

Reference Fried Chicken Restaurant Visit: Please take careful note of the time taken to deliver your order. DO NOT USE A STOPWATCH.

The mind boggles. Can you imagine the reaction of staff if you were to time the arrival of your food with a stopwatch and then whip out your thermometer and carefully test its temperature?

Even us morons aren't that stupid.

So . . . how do you make a 'complete idiot' of yourself doing something so seemingly easy? Well, mistakes have been made. One particular visit went so completely wrong I can't believe I ever had another. Come to think of it, I haven't had another.

On a visit to one family pub-cum-restaurant, I seemed to completely forget I was supposed to conceal my reasons for visiting. In fact, I have no idea what I was playing at – the beer must have kicked in early – I seemed to forget everything about everything. Therefore, when Lorraine whispered across the table, 'Can I order anything on the menu?', I boomed back, 'YES, JUST PRETEND YOU'RE OUT FOR A MEAL.'

Lorraine looked at me in horror. This rather peculiar comment raised heads on tables all around us. One old chap asked his wife, quite loudly, what I'd said.

'He's saying to pretend they're out for a meal, dear.'

'What? Well . . . they are, aren't they?'

'I don't know, dear. That's all he said.'

I sat in silence for a moment, trying to ascertain whether any members of staff had heard me.

Just when I thought I'd composed myself and put my mouth back into gear, I got up from the table and loudly announced, 'I'LL GO AND HAVE A LOOK AT THE TOILETS.'

I headed for the lavatories with every head following me. I noted that Lorraine's was the only exception. Her head was firmly in her hands.

Minutes later, after ordering meals at the bar, I realised I'd forgotten to read the barmaid's name badge. Anybody with half a brain would have left it at that. Instead I returned to the bar, conspicuously pretending to study the optics, and shot a clandestine glance at her badge.

I couldn't make out her name. I squinted. Still no good. Completely forgetting the need to be subtle, I squinted hard and leant forward, quickly becoming aware that both the girl in question, whom I now knew to be named Juliana, and her manager were watching me in astonishment. Clicking back to reality far too late, I realised that I appeared to be openly staring at Juliana's fairly exposed chest in a disturbingly squinty-eyed, pervy way. I smiled, trying to think of something to say. They both stared at me. I edged away, my cheeks burning red with embarrassment, and sat heavily down at our table.

Lorraine noted my unease and asked what was wrong. By way of rounding off the worst secret mission ever I blurted out, again much, much too loudly, 'IT WAS AWFUL. I WAS TRYING TO

GET THE BARMAID'S NAME, BUT EVERYONE THOUGHT I WAS LOOKING DOWN HER TOP.'

And so you see, now you think of market research as quite a romantic job, don't you?

But when I do feel the need for help, Brum and Maya are always there for me. Brum you know all about, but it's quite extraordinary the embarrassment levels a toddler can take you to. Sure, I'd had plenty of exposure to toddler embarrassment already, but nothing compared to my summer onslaught.

Maya chooses her situations well. She prefers crowded places like pubs, where there're lots of people and so maximum embarrassment potential. Not that she hangs out in pubs often – she can't reach the bar – but I'd started taking her for early evening pints with a friend of mine named Pete. I'd been meeting up with Pete on a Thursday early evening for the past decade or so, and the fact I now had Maya with me didn't seem any reason to stop. Not until she gave me one, anyway. Or two. First she turned me into a beggar, then she committed a serious attack on an innocent bystander.

I think the 'beggar' thing was deliberate. Maya stood on a stool to admire a pub fruit machine up close. I wouldn't let her feed it, claiming to have no money. A group of women brushed by and Maya, grabbing one of the group's attention, and also her coat, hurriedly explained our predicament.

In true Dickensian style she held out an upturned palm, looking all sad and mournful, and said, 'Please can we have some monies. My daddy hasn't got any monies.'

To complete the picture she rested a tiny, dirty hand (chocolate) on my shoulder and looked as if she was about to cry.

I smiled at first, but my smile quickly faded when two of the women started rooting around in their handbags.

'No . . . no,' I started to say.

One of them gave me 50p.

Then they were gone, through the door and into the car park. Pete arrived seconds later. He looked around the room in a puzzled kind of way.

Finally he looked at me.

'Are you the only two in here?' he said in a low, conspiratorial voice.

'Yes . . . why . . . what are you going to do?'

'Eh? Do? Nothing. It's just I heard some women in the car park saying some bloke in here should be ashamed of himself . . . must've been something to do with the landlord.'

Brilliant. Not only a beggar, but one who uses his child to do the dirty work. A career move involving Maya in rag clothing and Brum in bandages entered my mind and was instantly dismissed.

Pete has eyed that landlord with deep suspicion ever since.

Believe it or not, that wasn't the first time I've been caught embezzling at a fruit machine.

I once sat down at a table in a seaside café and noticed that the fruit machine was showing more than fifty credits. I nudged Lorraine and she looked at the machine in a totally uninterested sort of way. I tried to do likewise and lose interest in the thing but I couldn't. There was no one else in the café – just the owner, who seemed equally uninterested, and, you know . . . FIFTY credits. That was interesting.

I stood up and studied the machine. Nobody rushed from a dark corner to claim their unused credits, which came to over ten pounds' worth. I tentatively pushed the flashing start button and the three wheels spun. I pressed again. The lights flashed crazily. I had nudges. I got excited, leaning forward and straining to see right up the reels. At this point a red face sporting glasses and a moustache popped round the side of the machine as if from nowhere. I was crouching and yet we were nose to nose.

He looked at me as if I were something Sammy had dragged in and said nothing. And then he was gone. I stared at the spot his face had occupied seconds earlier. Strange. Very strange indeed. But he'd said absolutely nothing about the credits, so I pressed nudge. And again. And again.

'WILL YOU BLOODY WELL PACK THAT IN!' boomed a voice from behind the machine, so loud that Lorraine almost choked on her pasty. 'You'll have my sodding fingers off!'

What?

I looked round the side of the machine. The bespectacled, moustachioed face met me halfway at waist height. I stared down, he stared up. He was on his knees sucking his finger. Lorraine glanced over and did a double-take – the situation was looking a little too erotic.

'Pack it in, will you,' he muttered, and crawled off behind the machine.

I tentatively glanced around the back. The machine had it's back-plate off. The strange face with the grazed finger was now busily doing something to it with a screwdriver. It glanced at me and glowered.

I grinned sheepishly and edged back to my table.

'Faulty machine, Repair Man?' mumbled Lorraine, without even looking up, a suppressed laugh now becoming the latest cause of pasty-choking.

Anyway, my main reason for meeting up with Pete in the pub, other than beer, was to play pool. Maya's 'sweep and destroy' attitude to pool tables soon put a stop to that particular pleasure, and I began to wonder whether I should maybe forget about Thursday teatimes at the pub during the Mayan summer. The 'sockosaurus attack' put the issue beyond doubt.

In a vain bid to keep Maya amused at the bar, Pete had taken her spare socks from her backpack and placed them on her hands, telling her they were both dinosaurs and naming them Dave and Colin (obviously – I expect 'Dave and Colin' would instantly spring to most people's minds as dinosaur names. Try it. Ask a friend to name three dinosaurs. Chances are they'll say Tyrannosaurus Rex, Dave and Colin).

Maya spent a deliriously happy five minutes slamming her growling sock-puppets into one another before deciding not to be selfish and to bring others into her fun game. And so, with a mighty roar, Colin suddenly swooped upwards and punched a passing stranger's testicles with quite considerable force. The poor chap threw beer over all and sundry as Pete and I reacted with the agility of open-mouthed cardboard cut-outs. There was just time to hear the shocking words 'LOOK OUT, DAVE'S GONNA GET YOU!' before the stranger received a second terrible uppercut from Maya's rocket left.

Bidding Pete farewell until the autumn, I narrowed Maya's options considerably.

But at least all these things happened out of Lorraine's worried gaze. Lorraine feels that they *only* happened because they were out of her worried gaze, but she's not immune. If ever a day contained as many negative incidents as our family day out at the 'Goat Centre', a local wildlife park housing all sorts of animals but with (funnily enough) an awful lot of goats, then I'd like to know about it. Admittedly, nothing was in any way her fault, and in some cases it was quite clearly my fault, but her worried gaze didn't *stop* any of it, did it?

Things got off to an incredibly bad start when, within seconds of stepping through the turnstiles, I decked Maya with an abrupt cuff to the ear. What the crowd of startled onlookers didn't see was the wasp that'd settled on the ear in question, and which my determined smack had missed by quite some way. Thus, to all intents and purposes, it looked as if I'd suddenly turned around and brutally slapped a toddler to the ground with a shout of 'LOOK OUT' for no apparent reason.

Lorraine, who thankfully saw the wasp and knew my actions to have been clumsy rather than those of a crazy man, helped Maya to her feet, brushed her down and insisted she didn't retaliate.

It really wasn't Maya's day. No more than two minutes later she got headbutted by a goat.* Maya spotted the cute kid, which was deemed safe enough to wander among the park's visitors, and ran towards it waving her newly acquired bag of goat food. The goat spotted the not-so-cute Maya-kid running straight at it, and charged forward to meet her head-on. The resulting collision was much easier on the goat.

Maya keeled over backwards, absolutely poleaxed. For a

---

*I told Pete about this. Unbelievably, in response he muttered miserably, 'That's always happening to me, that is.'

moment we thought she was out cold. She stared at the sky for a few seconds and then her brows furrowed. But anger, not tears, followed. She bounded to her feet, and ran at the retreating goat – so quickly that my only option was to down her with a rugby tackle.

Onlookers who'd witnessed me clout Maya round the head now watched me bring her crashing to the ground by way of 'taking her legs out' in mid-stride. The looks on their faces seemed to convey the general opinion that I needed very urgent psychiatric help.

Any lingering doubts must surely have been dispelled by my behaviour during lunch at the 'Happy Goat Café'.

As we worked our way in single file through a maze of tightly packed tables, me clutching a trayful of Billy's Big Bite Burgers and Nanny's Nifty Nibbles, I completely failed to miss an old lady's precariously placed chair leg and pitched forward. All that lay between me and an undignified collapse to the floor was an oblivious Maya walking ahead of me. With one hand on my tray I slammed the palm of the other down on Maya's head. Maya made a valiant attempt to support my weight, immediately crumpling to her knees. But she'd been enough to keep me upright, if not slow my momentum. I quickly splayed my legs, sailed over her and slammed my tray down on the nearest table. Which didn't please its occupants at all.

Mumbling apologies, I glanced around at the sea of open-mouthed faces that warily watched. I was at it again – downing my daughter for the third time in a matter of hours and then leapfrogging over her head.

I sat down in embarrassed misery as an unfazed Maya began playing her games, holding a cup of milk to my face and repeating, 'Hello, I'm a cup' over and over until I finally cracked and smiled at her. Delighted, she shouted, 'Speak to the cup, Daddy, speak to the cup.'

'No, play with Mummy, Maya, I'm not . . .'

'Speak to the cup, Daddy, speak to the cup.'

'No, Maya, I'm . . .'

'Speak to the cup, speak to the cup.'

I sighed and gave in.

'Hello, cup,' I said.

'Don't you talk to me!' said the cup.

I looked at Lorraine, she looked at me, and we decided we'd best go home and see what Brum had been up to.

The Mousetrap

*'Cats like fighting mice. You get to keep your
looks fighting mice.'*

Timothy Gardener

'Do you sell humane mousetraps?'

'Hee hee!'

I stared uncertainly at the teenage girl serving me in our local DIY store. I'd asked what seemed a sensible question but received only a giggle for an answer.

'Er, do you sell them, then?'

'What?'

'Humane mousetraps.'

'Hee hee! What's a human mouse?'

'No, humane. A humane trap.'

This seemed to really do it. She laughed aloud for a few seconds and then asked, between giggles, 'For catching humans?!'

I sighed deeply. It was an effort of will to carry on.

'A humane trap. It catches mice without killing them.'

'Oh, OK. I'll show you where the mousetraps are. I think they're really cruel.'

'No, these ones aren't cruel. These ones catch mice alive and . . .'

'Well, I think they're cruel anyway.'

We arrived at the appropriate aisle, and the girl, who now considered me to be either a sadistic animal killer or a man who sets traps for humans, pointed at a row of lethal-looking mouse-traps. All had the words KILL or POISON emblazoned above pictures of teeth-baring rodents.

'There you go,' she said as she left me to it, 'I think they're really cruel.'

I went elsewhere and finally found what I was looking for. Lorraine had been very particular about the type of trap I bought. Not that I didn't agree. No sense in killing the poor little things when you could simply put them outside. On the other hand, neither should there be any need to buy a mousetrap when you have two full-grown cats at home.

Now Brum I can understand. Brum's the closest thing to an animal rights activist/vegetarian in the feline world. He won't hurt a fly. Flies hurt him. Sometimes badly. He's probably only a meat-eater because he can't read the ingredients on cat-food tins. Mind you, if, in his capacity as 'cat', he *could* read, it'd be out with the cat food and in with a life of smoked salmon, caviar and full-cream milk for the both of us. But Sammy? We've already established Sammy's normal-killer-cat status, and yet she does nothing. Outside the house, the mouse is her enemy, and more often than not her half-digested enemy. Inside – no interest at all. Not a flicker.

She no doubt started the problem in the first place – probably dragging a few mice in and forgetting to finish them off after a fun cuff-and-torture session. And Lorraine doesn't help matters by failing to encourage her. If Sammy shows so much as an iota of interest in the utility (mouse) room, Lorraine hauls her off to the lounge. In fact she won't even let Sammy sleep in the room, lest she kill mice in her sleep.

I set our humane trap with Brum by my side. It was a clever little thing (the trap, not Brum). The mice entered by a tunnel containing a weighted seesaw. Once inside, the seesaw flipped back and the exit closed. Not only was the trap humane, it offered refreshments. The captured mouse could eat its cheese bait while awaiting release.

Brum couldn't leave it alone. The smell of cheese had him totally captivated. He spent half his time sniffing the trap with a look of happy contentment on his face. The presence of a big fluffy tabby at the trap's entrance wasn't going to promote rapid mouse capture.

Eventually we caught one. Whether the mouse slipped under Brum to reach its objective I don't know, but during the night the trap became occupied. Brum peered at the box and a pair of beady black eyes peered back. I picked up the trap and flicked the catch to take a closer look.

Why don't I ever read instruction books? Why didn't I see the huge footnote, 'HOLD TRAP AWAY FROM YOU WHEN RELEASING CATCH'?

The door swung open and a flying mouse hit me between the eyes. I dropped the trap in panic. Four unexpected bonus mice scurried out. Brum squealed in alarm and backed into a corner. For a brief, amazing moment, Brum was cornered by four tiny mice, one of whom stood on its hind legs and studied him.

Then they were gone; pattering over an unopened gazebo box marked PRIORITY, and back into the dark gaps beneath our cupboards. Brum stared in horror at the space the standing mouse had occupied. He remained staring for quite some time.

The following day Maya decided to assist. She could do no worse than Brum and me, so I allowed her to scatter cheese on the utility-room floor and stand holding our laundry basket in patient expectation.

Within two minutes, she came running into the living room screaming, 'I GOT ONE, DADDY, I GOT ONE, DADDY!'

I followed my ecstatic daughter through the house, with Sammy following close behind to see what all the fuss was about. I reached the utility room and found the laundry basket upside down on the floor. I knelt down and looked inside. A pair of big green eyes stared back at me.

She'd caught Brum.

The biggest rodent in the house sat happily munching cheese in his toddler-made cat-trap, while his small cousins carried on their mousing business unhindered. This was typical. I suddenly felt the urge to sit under a nice safe basket myself.

My mind was made up. I'd go and see the girl in the DIY store. Maybe she could offer me a discount on a human trap.

Marinating Rites

*'You should never have your best trousers on
when you go out to fight for freedom.'*

Henrik Ibsen

O n a scorcher of an August Sunday, I sat on the patio and watched Maya splashing happily in her paddling pool. I'd dearly liked to have joined her in that sparkling cool water but, bearing in mind Maya's aforementioned attitude to 'paddling pool sharing', I'd rather have got in with a great white shark.

So while Maya enjoyed exclusive bathing rights, I sat perspiring in a deckchair, chatting (quarrelling) with her and watching red kites in the distance. Lorraine had nipped indoors to make a phone call and the cats were both sleeping – Sammy next to a bedroom fan and Brum flat out on the baking-hot garden wall above my head. There was that still-air gentle noise about the day, the chirp of insects, the song of birds, the buzz of distant planes and the snoring of a sparked-out tabby.

Wherever and whenever Brum sleeps, he *really* sleeps. It's a known fact that cats come back to full alertness faster than any other creature[*] but there's no 'alert cat half-awake awareness' about Brum. His lights go well and truly out. And so, there's an element of danger when Brum nods off atop a high wall . . .

I'd just taken a sip of ice-cool Coke, and Maya was busily performing the apparently essential task of filling an armada of floating plastic teacups from a giant plastic teapot. Above her head, Brum yawned, stretched, rolled over on to his back, carried on rolling and rolled off the wall.

---

[*]This is hardly surprising. One of the ingredients in most cat foods is taurine, an essential nutrient for feline well being. As taurine is the stuff they use in Red Bull and the like, the only surprise is that cats ever sleep at all, never mind for seventeen hours a day.

Coke fizzed down my nostrils as I watched in horror. Brum dropped through the air like a brick – that daft contented smile of sleep still on his face, his eyes tight shut and legs outstretched. His eyes shot open a millisecond before he hit the water with tremendous force, causing a huge tidal wave to sweep mercilessly across the pool and smash down on an unsuspecting Maya.

Teacups flew into the air in an explosion of water, plastic saucers splashed over the sides, a rubber duck completed an aerial somersault before bumping down on Maya's soaked head.

Seconds after initial impact, the real shock waves began. A wide-eyed tabby surfaced in panic, only to have his head bob up into an overturned transparent bucket. Maya finished rubbing water from her eyes and the first thing she saw was Brum, not only in her pool yet again, but brazenly leering at her through scuffed perspex. She was on him in a microsecond, beating his plastic helmet with her tiny fists.

Through Coca-Cola tears I watched Maya attempt to haul the bucket from Brum's head, only for its handle to catch firmly under his chin. As Brum tried to wade in the opposite direction, Maya pulled harder still, causing the trapped handle to drop down and loop around Brum's neck. She gave one last, mighty tug, dragging Brum up and backwards by the throat. The bucket's handle suddenly snapped free and a half-throttled cat splashed heavily back into the water.

Finally finding my voice, I bellowed out to Maya to stop killing Brum, loudly reminding her that we must never hit cats or blokes with tattoos.

Lorraine had been gone only ten minutes, and yet returned to a previously harmonious scene to find Brum standing, drenched and unmoving, half in and half out of the paddling pool, and me stumbling forward to hold back a screaming Maya, absolutely beside herself with rage and still trying to smack him with her bucket.

Maya ran to Lorraine as if rescued, and Brum and I stood there, him in the water, me beside him, both looking at each other in silence and wondering how we could best have handled things differently.

'Why's Brum in the pool?' asked Lorraine calmly. 'You know how Maya feels about that pool.'

I certainly did. And Brum did too. He'd been beaten and garrotted for Maya's views.

But toddlers' opinions can change suddenly and dramatically, and Maya now started whooping with joy, pointing and singing, 'Brum's having a bath, Brum's having a bath!' He looked up at her despairingly and then, as if Maya's taunts had reminded him that he was standing in a paddling pool, he slowly struggled out.

Something must have lodged in that little head of hers, because a week later, on an equally hot Sunday, she gave Brum another bath. A pretty nasty bath really, in a jar of rancid pickled-onion vinegar. Difficult for a cat to climb into? He didn't have to. Maya emptied the entire contents of the jar over the unsuspecting Brum as he sat waiting for his lunch.

I think he'd probably have fancied something more along the lines of a nice piece of roast chicken or a smoked salmon fillet, maybe a shoulder of lamb, but certainly not half a litre of foul-smelling vinegar (or for that matter the sloppy-jelly tinned cat food he was about to get).

When a shocked Brum evaded legs and grabbing hands to escape through the open back door without his paws touching the ground, I wondered whether he'd even considered the consequences of basking in hot sunshine while basted from head to paw in vinegar. It was the long-suffering Dave who first sniffed the air and realised something wasn't right.

Dave was having a barbecue, and the rancid stench of deep-frying pickling fluids and wet cat fur didn't do much for his guests' appetites. He could barely believe that the cat lying on his lawn, over twenty feet away, could possibly have been responsible for the pungent odour enveloping his patio. But he forced himself to believe it, immediately and without question, simply because the cat was Brum. Dave kindly passed the offending article over the hedge, at arm's length, and suggested he might need sorting out. Whether he meant this in practical terms, or was demanding Brum be beaten up, I don't know.

We're still talking about life in England, by the way, in case I'm giving a Mediterranean feel by mentioning so many sunny days in one summer. Where we live, as in most of the country, more often than not it's either raining or about to rain, and when it rains Brum acts more or less the same way he does in thirty-degree sunshine. He stays out in the open and gets soaked. The only difference is he stands up in rain and lies down in sunshine, which may point to a genetic kinship with cattle, who are also known to lie or sit depending on the prevalent weather systems. There is a possibility, then, that Maya spotted something in those lions that the scientific community has been missing for years.

Whether that's nonsense or not,[*] Brum is definitely an all-weather cat. He'll just go outside and get roasted, saturated, frozen or blown to bits – he doesn't care which as long as he's out there, facing whatever nature can throw at him; fighting the elements and losing every time. But he does care, passionately, about Maya's fondness for marinating him, and would prefer she didn't. The vinegar was followed by drenchings in milk, bubble bath, orange juice and, worst of all, apple juice. I don't know what they put in cartons of apple juice (probably apple juice) but it reeks something awful – a sort of ammonia-like smell, not unlike cat pee in

[*] Nonsense.

fact. I'm sure anybody who met him that day would have instantly assumed he'd pissed himself.

Maya's marinating habit may simply be a case of carrying forward a family tradition, which brings me to someone who hasn't been mentioned all that much so far – chiefly because, like Sammy, he never actually does anything – Lorraine's father, Maya's Granddad Walt, or Gandalf Stick as Maya renamed him (he has a walking stick, he's a proper granddad, or Gandalf. He even has a tweed flat cap, white moustache and spectacles – he's the real deal).

Gandalf will very readily attest to our family marinating rites, because although he doesn't ever do anything, he seems to very often be on the receiving end of our doings.

It's become a bit of a family joke that whenever he goes out, one of us seems to spill a drink over him. Myself particularly. As he's Lorraine's dad, I show him all the reverence and respect required from a son-in-law, and I do this by regularly sloshing hot coffee down his trousers or throwing beer over his shirt. I don't know why, I just can't seem not to. He's like a drinks magnet.

This is an example of a typical Gandalf Stick week. Perhaps not entirely typical, because he doesn't always subject himself to staying with us for the week, but a typical week with us at least.

On his first evening with us, we took him to a local pub. Within seconds of my sitting down and fielding a few gazebo timescale queries, I changed the subject abruptly by lurching across the table for a menu and punching a full pint of cider into Gandalf's lap. Gandalf reacted positively, jerking forward and sloshing his own pint into his face. Lorraine and Maya found this hilarious, of course, particularly when, frothy beer dripping from his moustache, he complained that cider was seeping into his socks.

To make matters worse, when he set off to clean himself up in the toilets, Maya alerted the entire pub to his predicament by yelling, 'HAVE YOU WET YOURSELF, GANDALF?' which didn't please him at all. Every face in the room instantly turned and stared in shock at his dripping-wet trousers.

I don't know whether it's something to do with the apples, but cider can smell a bit like urine as well, can't it? Many of the pub regulars certainly gave the impression that they thought so.

You should never laugh out loud at something a toddler says if you don't want them to repeat it. Toddlers don't understand the concept of an old joke. If it's told once and it got a laugh, it should get a laugh every time it's told.[*]

Therefore, Maya's catchphrase for the week became 'Have you wet yourself, Gandalf'. Always delivered at high volume, always in a crowded place, always instigating startled glances and muffled chuckles. The poor old bloke couldn't go anywhere without all and sundry believing him to be incontinent, particularly as he usually had a big wet patch on his trousers. In a tearoom, I did the honours by chucking lemonade at him; over the course of a five-mile car journey Maya doused the usual area with orange juice every twenty-five yards or so (by way of celebrating each and every one of our town's hundred-odd speed bumps) and even Brum got in on the act, falling asleep on his lap and drooling copiously down his inside leg.

And these were only incidents relating to his trousers. His shirts fared no better. At breakfast I shook a bottle of tomato ketchup without realising the lid was loose, splattering his shirt so suddenly and so thoroughly that Lorraine thought he'd been shot.

And if he thought things could get no worse, it was all as nothing compared to his last evening with us. He'd packed his holdall and left it in the spare bedroom, and settled down with Lorraine to watch TV. Maya was in bed and I thought I'd catch up with things in the office. Office is a bit grand, because the office is just a desk and computer in the spare bedroom – Gandalf's bedroom.

As is his habit, Brum jumped on to the desk and settled down beside my arm. We'd been there no more than a minute when Brum suddenly gave a huge groaning belch and vomited over the side of the desk. With Sod's law in full operation, the whole lot

[*]Brum's Solid Universe Theory.

splurged down into Gandalf's open holdall like a great lumpy waterfall.

I stared in disbelief for a second. I thought about zipping up the holdall and saying nothing – just letting Gandalf find the stinking mess when he got home. How could I tell him that, after a week of regularly soaking and staining his clothes, we'd now gone the whole hog and soiled the whole ruddy lot at once?

I couldn't. I called Lorraine into the room and silently pointed at Gandalf's holdall. She stared for some time, as if trying to take in exactly what it was she was looking at. Eventually, Lorraine strode off back to the lounge and I heard the words 'Got some bad news, I'm afraid', as Brum and I quietly slipped out the back door.

When he got back to the safety and comfort of his own home, he must finally have achieved the sense of 'getting away from it all' that we'd promised all along. I think that, all in all, had he actually been shot, he'd have had a much better week.

The Most Peculiar Case of the Seaside Village and Its Missing Cats

'Strange to you,
Stranger to me,
Those barbaric folk who
Live by the sea'

Stuart Graham

There comes a time in every stay-at-home man's life, or summer, when he must get away from his cat.

That time had come. It was time to go on holiday. We set off for Wells-next-the-Sea in Norfolk, not only hoping that the resort would be significantly better than its daft name, but also that Dave next door would be able to handle Brum. It was his brief, for one week only, to feed and 'keep an eye on' our one and a half cats. Dave is a brave man.

There was no way Brum was coming with us. Wells-next-the-Sea is only next-the-sea for part of each day. At high tide it's a pretty seaside village, at low tide it's a pretty village next to a salt marsh. Wells actually looks great whether the view is marshland or sea, but the fact that marsh becomes sea so bloody rapidly means that, had we brought him, one minute Brum could have been happily skipping on sand dunes and hiding from seagulls (Brum-next-the sea), the next desperately paddling for Holland (Brum-in-the-sea).

As we approached Wells after a 'lovely' five-hour journey, a roadside sign convinced us beyond doubt that we'd made the right decision in leaving the cats at home:

CATS' EYES REMOVED

read the shocking inscription. What?! What sort of company offers a service like that?! While totally appreciating that the people of Norfolk may well find it necessary to remove their cats' eyes now and then, you'd hardly expect somebody to make an industry of the barbaric practice. I could see we were going to have trouble in Wells-next-the-Sea.

But the week passed pleasantly enough. There were no

desperate text messages from Dave, nothing about him on the news and no reports of any huge explosions in the Wycombe area. He was evidently coping.

Neither was there any local evidence of a cat mutilation culture. Indeed, we were awoken by the terrible screeching miaows of a cat having its eyes removed not once. After five days we realised why. It was Maya who first noticed. 'Where's Brum?' she asked over breakfast.

'At home,' Lorraine told her. 'With Sammy.'

'Why there no other Brums?'

I flinched involuntarily. Other Brums. What a horrible thought. Then it hit me. I hadn't seen another Brum in five days. In fact, I hadn't seen any cats at all. During almost a week in Wells, I hadn't seen one single cat, not even in the quayside toilets when the fishing boats were in.

No cats? Was the cats'-eyes sign for real? Where were they all? A village without cats? A *fishing* village without cats? Impossible.

During the next two days I made it my business to find one. I looked down every garden path, glanced at every window, gazed up at every rooftop. Nothing. Not a single feline face stared back at me. Just a few disturbed locals.

On our last day in Wells I asked a café owner about the lack of local cat life. She seemed not to understand.

'Are there no cats in Wells?'

'Sorry, love. How do you mean?'

'Cats? I've seen no cats here.'

'I haven't got a cat, love.'

'Has anyone in Wells got a cat? I haven't seen a cat in a week.'

She seemed perplexed that I'd want to.

'Oh . . . well, never mind,' she said. 'Are you off home today?'

What was this? Why hadn't she answered my question? What sinister thing was afoot?

I tried again.

'Are there any cats in Wells? Any at all?'

'Oh,' she said, her face setting into something between a scowl and a grimace, 'they're here alright.'

And that was it. She went off to serve another customer, leaving me absolutely certain she wasn't a cat lover, but otherwise totally bewildered.

I'd given up on seeing a Wells cat or discovering the truth about their absence as we pulled down the drive of our rented cottage and headed for home. Then I saw something unexpected. The man in the cottage next door was emptying a cat-litter tray into his dustbin. I screeched to a halt and wound down my window.

'HAVE YOU GOT A CAT?' I called.

The man looked at me, looked pointedly at the litter tray in his hand, smirked and nodded. Duh . . . yeah . . . that's why I'm holding a litter tray, you idiot, was the unspoken inference. I couldn't think what to say next.

The man retreated through his door, probably realising for the first time the calibre of the people who'd been living at number two for a week. I stared fixedly at my steering wheel, red in the cheeks and trying to ignore Lorraine, who was shaking her head beside me. Worse still was the realisation that I'd spent an entire week looking for signs of cat life while living next door to a cat.

As I pulled away I glanced over my shoulder. The cat in question stared back at me from the man's window. And it stared at me with two big, shiny green eyes.

Skater Frog

'Nobly wild, not mad.'
Robert Herrick

I think I've discovered Brum's intellectual double.

A frog hopped into the garden the other day, just as Brum emerged from under a bush. The frog stopped dead and stared at Brum. Brum stopped in mid-stride and stared at the frog. Neither moved for at least a minute. A profound psychological battle was under way.

Suddenly, the frog hopped a foot in the air, landing exactly where he'd taken off. Brum's hackles rose, his back arched. And then he too jumped a foot in the air, all four legs leaving the ground at once, and landed back on the same spot.

An edgy frog regarded a scruffy tabby. The frog jumped a foot in the air. The moment he landed, Brum shot into the air. Brum landed, the frog jumped. The frog landed, Brum jumped. The frog jumped again, Brum jumped again. It was if the pair were on an invisible seesaw. It was one of the most ridiculous sights I've ever seen, and thanks to Brum I've seen a few.

If mimicry is the sincerest form of flattery, then Brum was in awe of his amphibian foe. The encounter ended when a bored frog hopped away and left a shaken Brum standing alone on the lawn. I was left crying with laughter, as I so often am in Brum's company.

Something about that 'jump-off' reminded me of two lads I'd once seen, doing more or less the same thing on skateboards. From a standing position, first one would launch into the air on his board, then the other. Each would land on the board, teeter for a moment and then wait his turn to jump again. This procedure continued until one of them broke his ankle.

The comparison is no surprise. Brum loves skateboarding. Brum skateboards with craft and elegance, and differs from other skateboarders in only one respect. He doesn't use a board.

Brum is extremely inventive when it comes to his 'boarding'. He will use any highly polished or wet surface he can find, and then hurtle across it on all fours until he comes to a natural stop. Like a wall.

Not surprisingly, his skateboarding career has provided us with one of his silliest accidents. He jumped from the floor one day, hitting a kitchen worktop absolutely covered in surface water and so very, very slippery.

Assuming classic skateboarder's pose, he skidded straight along the worktop like a saloon-bar delivery, never even looking like stopping as he plunged backside first into a sink full of steaming-hot water and crockery. His mouth opened wide in sheer heat shock as he thrashed his way out, all the time miaowing and shrieking like a banshee.

The carnage was admirable. He broke three out of six dinner plates, drenched the kitchen floor and broke a glass. He then ran full pelt, head down into the living room, spinning the advancing Maya off her feet and putting her flat on her back. Maya howled with delight and, finding her feet, chased Brum three times round the living room before the pair of them decided there were probably enough Fairy Liquid bubbles in the air.

And his skater-dude, couldn't-care-less attitude to life and worktops doesn't stop there. Absolutely not. Barely a month into my self-imposed summer of strife, Brum demonstrated this fact perfectly by attempting to nonchalantly commit hara-kiri on those very surfaces.

It may simply have been because I'd been home all summer that he felt the sudden urge to carry out a 'most honourable suicide'. It may even have been in reaction to growing gazebo tension. But I doubt it. In fact, I think it was me he originally intended to sort out. At least he gave that impression when, for some reason, he decided to stalk me.

I was at one end of the worktop, he at the other. I caught his aggressive stance from the corner of my eye. Head down, eyes wide, ears back, tail wagging, back low to the worktop. He edged towards me, slowly, steadily, menacingly.

If it were possible to advertise a stalked approach more thoroughly, I really don't know how.

Within two stealthy steps, he flipped a plate by treading heavily on its raised edge, instantly covering himself in gravy and triggering a series of loud clatters and clunks. By this time, you'd think he'd have had an inkling that I was aware of his advance. But no. He kept coming, gravy dripping off his nose, still stalking, still seeming to believe I had no idea he was poised to strike. A spoon fell to the floor, followed by a knife. The kitchen-roll holder fell sideways against the window. Another plate was skilfully non-avoided, only this one had a sharp kitchen knife hanging over its edge. Brum trod on the very tip of the knife's handle, upending it through 180 degrees and causing the blade to point briefly upwards . . . just long enough for Brum to take one last lethal step forward and pin it in place with his throat.

At this point he stopped dead.

He stood there, absolutely still, his head tilting up and backwards in horror, eyes moving slowly down to the sharp point pressed under his chin. I tried to move slowly, tried to edge forward without startling him, in order to remove this extremely dangerous item before he impaled himself on it. He, of course, thought I'd turned the tables and was now stalking him.

As I carefully grasped the knife's handle, he took an angry swipe at me. I instinctively jerked my hand, narrowly missing Brum's face with a swift blade-slash. Brum swiped at me again. The whole thing suddenly took on the appearance of a knife fight. I flipped the knife from one hand to the other, very much in the tradition of *West Side Story*. Brum edged warily sideways, ready to spring forward. I could almost hear the music and feel the tension.

At this point I realised we had an audience. It was Maria . . . no, Maya – sorry. I carefully pointed the knife away from Brum. Maya looked at me quizzically. I smiled at her.

'Why are you hitting Brummy with a knife?' she enquired.

'I'm not. I wasn't. We were just . . .' I spluttered, fervently hoping that she wouldn't remember this scene in years to come. An image of her lying on a psychiatrist's couch flashed through my mind. 'My earliest memories of my father were of him knife-fighting cats in our kitchen.'

Or worse, what if she mentioned the incident to Lorraine, who was already having serious misgivings about my ability to look after Maya? Tales of sharp-bladed nursery horseplay with the pets wouldn't help.

Brum saw my distraction and seized his opportunity with four sharp sets of claws. He lunged forward, grabbed my arm extremely painfully and sunk his teeth in.

I knifed him.

Or at least, I sort of did. How I didn't kill him I'll never know (I'll get him next time). It was an automatic reaction. I just tried to grab him but stabbed forward with the knife. It came so close to spearing him that it ended up coated in a huge clump of tabby fur.

Maya watched in awe as the tussle ended, the only blood shed being mine, as usual. I dragged my scratched hand from Brum's wicked grip and ushered him to the floor. He marched to the cat-flap in a huff and forgot how to do the next bit. I examined my raked hand. If you're beginning to get the impression that Brum and I fight quite a lot of the time, then you're wrong. We fight all the time. But Brum generally only attacks me, thankfully. Not Maya, not Lorraine, not other cats, not even . . . frogs.

Just me. I think it stems from our play fights when we were kittens, or rather when he was. He thinks it's fine to fight my hands – not my face, just my hands. He seems to see the two things as entirely different entities, not in any way connected to the same brain. Which is probably a fairly astute assumption for a cat.

Maya watched me thoughtfully for a few seconds and then walked back to the living room.

Five hours later she told Lorraine I'd hit Brum with a knife.

The Missing Link

*'Cats and monkeys – monkeys and cats – all
human life is there!'*

James Henry

lthough it would explain a lot, there is no hereditary link between my father and my cat. Which is surprising.

You see, although I blame Brum (often correctly) for the constant round of mishaps and disasters that befall our family, I'm well aware, as I think you probably are by now, that I'm as much to blame as he is. And I'm as much to blame as he is for one reason – Dad. Dad passed all that he is straight down to me like a bucket of cold porridge. Meet Brian Pascoe, aged seventy – humanity's answer to Brum. Dad and Brum would appear to have been cut from the same cloth. They have an almost frightening amount in common. Knockouts, fires, humiliations – Dad's life mirrors Brum's uncannily. Although I will say Dad has so far avoided fur-balls, fleas and an urge to claim property by urinating over it. I think.

Dad is just as bad as Brum, probably even worse. He grew up during the war, the son of a Portsmouth fire-fighter who was blown thirty feet in the air by a German bomb but still managed to amuse startled onlookers by continuing to pedal his rickety old pushbike in mid-air, right down to a very unpleasant landing that he somehow survived. I'd like to have known my grandfather better; he sounds . . . familiar. The fact that Dad was born in what was to be one of the most heavily bombed cities in the world makes his luck only marginally better than poor Brum's with Slough.

And at least one poet thought Slough deserved the same sort of treatment – to quote John Betjeman:

> *Come, friendly bombs, and fall on Slough!*
> *It isn't fit for humans now,*
> *There isn't grass to graze a cow.*
> *Swarm over, Death!*

That's nice, isn't it? He didn't mention whether it was fit for felines, of course. Depends on his view on cats, I suppose.

Truthfully, Brum was born in much better times. OK, so Slough and 'good times' aren't often found in the same sentence, but anything had to be better than the prospect of Messerschmitts landing in your spare bedroom.

It was in later years that Brum's likenesses to Dad became brutally apparent. Their most noticeable similarity (apart from the ears) is a refusal to accept the existence of glass.

Once upon a time, in a crowded pub named the Ferry at Cookham, Dad ushered his family to an outdoor riverside table and purchased a tray full of drinks and crisps at the bar. Carefully striding through the pub like an out-of-control juggernaut, loaded tray in hand, he walked straight into a plate-glass window.

With a huge bang and the crash of broken glasses, he rebounded backwards into a wall and slumped to the floor. I have never been so embarrassed in all my life.

The whole pub saw it happen and everybody looked at us when Mum rushed inside to assist the bar staff in consoling him. At twelve years old, whether he felt OK or not didn't bother me half as much as the fact that I was in some way associated with this lunatic.

Around a decade later, Brum was at it too.

From the word go, Brum has had major issues with glass. He simply can't see it. Brum will walk into windows that have been in place for ten years.

And it's not only windows. Brum has the same problem with all glass, including mirrors, which is incredible. How can you fail to see a mirror? To be unable to spot a mirror until you've

walked face first into it is very odd indeed. This begs the question – is it the mirror he can't see . . . or himself? The very fact that he can walk into a wall-hanging mirror without even breaking stride proves that he is at least perceiving a reflected room, and attempting to walk into it. What he can't be seeing is the furry-faced arrangement of pointy ears and whiskers coming in the opposite direction. Brum is therefore one of the few people I know who is constantly surprised to 'bump into' himself. Neither can he see people in mirrors. If I stand in a position out of Brum's direct vision, and wave at his reflection in a mirror he's facing, he should by all rights see me and respond in some way. He doesn't flinch.

Mentioning this, of course, provides yet more ammunition for those who find my behaviour increasingly odd, but would also seem to prove that while Brum sees mirrors as simple doors, he rejects the notion that they can in any way support life.

Brum's window dilemma is much more serious than his mirror-people snubbing. So much so that he once broke a window with his head. The window in question was at my old bachelor flat. Inside the window was my kitchen, outside was a flat roof running up to the window.

One summer day, Brum came springing from dustbin to fence to flat roof in an amazingly agile way ('amazingly agile' had he been born a moose) and didn't break stride at all upon spotting me at the window and heading straight for me.

I didn't register alarm at first. I do seem to remember that in the last moments before impact I wondered why Brum appeared to be rapidly gaining pace. Only as he connected did I realise he had no intention of stopping.

I still don't really know how he could have broken the entire window. Granted, he has an extremely hard head, and I realise that a sixteen-pound missile has every chance of breaking windows, but he's only a cat . . . they're simply not built for demolition work. He should have hit it and glanced elegantly off sideways. Not hit it full-on with a splintering crash. The window simply disintegrated. I jumped backwards in shock as glass rained down around me. The noise was deafening – glass shattered and smashed everywhere; the room was instantly transformed into a sea of broken shards.

When the thundering pandemonium subsided, a lone cat stood picturesquely bordered by an empty wooden window frame.

And the Brum/Dad similarity doesn't end with window blindness. Throughout his life Brum has had an *almost* uniquely unfeline ability to knock himself out. Dad's good at that too.

He once misheard directions to a toilet and wandered down a long dark corridor in a pub whose name he's since completely forgotten, probably because of the ridiculously hard blow to the head he was about to receive.

He reached a heavy oak door, turned the handle and pulled. The last thing he remembers about the incident was a sense of almost superhuman power in his right arm. He wrenched that door right off its hinges and down on to his head with a skull-vibrating crack.

He could barely believe his own strength, but as they explained to him in the ambulance, the incident owed less to formidable strength than to the fact that the door wasn't secured in any way and was merely leaning against a brick wall. The paramedics seemed to find this very funny indeed, and were still chortling as they helped him into Casualty. Chortling gave way to hysterics as they attempted three times to explain what had happened to him. He finally had to tell the nurse himself, his two 'rescuers' holding their bellies and wiping tears from their cheeks.

Three weeks later, he did it again, although I really don't think it was entirely his fault. This time it happened in a cellar Guinness Bar in Soho Square, London. The toilet door had a huge sign warning you to mind the step. Consequently people walked through the door staring down at their feet and failed to notice that the overhead cistern was attached to a sloping, cave-like ceiling and so not overhead at all, but at forehead height just inside the door. He hit that thing so hard he bounced straight back into the pub and landed on his backside. The room roared with laughter and the barman put another chalk mark on the board. He was the fifth that night. Health and Safety was a fun thing before 'no win, no fee' lawyers, wasn't it?

What set Dad apart from his four predecessors, head and shoulders above them, in fact, was that he did it again two pints later, this time doing the job properly and passing out. He remembers very, very little about the rest of that evening, but I'm told the barman was concerned enough to put him in the recovery position before marking his blackboard. He was quite emotional apparently, never before having achieved six in an evening – a third of the total achieved by just one man. Pure genius!

Brum doesn't get out to pubs much, but if he did he'd probably be the best pub knockout artist in the world, and to prove it he added another brain-blanking blow to his own tally during the spring. It wasn't an elaborate affair. It was as if he realised that, as Brum, he has a job to do . . . and that job is to knock himself senseless. No messing, no thrills – just a case of getting in there and getting the thing done.

It was route-one stuff. He walked into the living room, tail in the air and full of the joys of the season, eyed our sideboard with sudden resolve, stood up on his hind legs, placed two paws carefully on its surface and . . . head-butted it with all his might.

Why would anybody, or any-cat, do something as moronic as that? Who, in their right mind, would walk into a room and simply head-butt a sideboard? He toppled backwards with his tongue hanging out of the side of his mouth, out for the count and with a serious headache on the way.

Job done.

An uncanny kinship is emerging, wouldn't you agree? Even stranger is the link between two incidents that occurred in the very same month. What are the chances of a seventy-year-old man and a cat being involved in separate accidents involving ensnarement and heavy blows to the genitals within two weeks of each other?

Not high, are they?

Particularly low in Brum's case, when you consider he's been neutered. But Brum wouldn't let a little thing like a lack of testicles hinder a decent disaster opportunity. Oh no! Not when he can render the blow to mine!

I'd loaded my car with boxes, paperwork and a toddler, and begun rolling back down my drive as I fiddled with my seat belt, when I caught sight of an unexpected tabby face in my rear-view mirror. Especially unexpected as it was inside the car, peering at the back of my head from the parcel shelf. He'd obviously jumped into the car at some point during loading. There was no way that furry little sod was coming out in the car with me. A whole range of vomit-related crash incidents flashed through my mind as I put my foot on the brake and opened my door.

I now realise that Brum was as eager to avoid a road trip with me as I was with him. The moment the door opened, he bounded from parcel shelf to rear seat to front-seat headrest to lap within the blink of the eye. A heavy moving lump with claws dropping where it hurts from three feet is not nice. Not nice at all. Things suddenly happened very quickly.

First, my whole body cramped up in excruciating pain; second, my foot abruptly left the brake; third, the car began rolling backwards with its door wide open; fourth, an escaping tabby launched a bid for freedom only to become entangled in my seat belt on his way to the tarmac; and lastly, the screaming tabby was dragged eight foot down the drive on his back by the runaway car.

Clutching my groin and choking back tears (something I often do), I finally managed to wrench the handbrake on. Ignoring Maya's jeers and laughter, I stumbled from the car and on to my knees to release a severely shocked Brum.

At this point I noticed Lorraine watching from an upstairs window. 'Nipping out to drop Maya at my mum's and run a few errands,' I'd said. Why then, ten minutes later, was the car skewered almost sideways across the drive, its driver doubled over holding his crotch and a wide-eyed cat lying prostrate on the floor? Lorraine gave a bemused shake of her head and disappeared from view.

You may well be wondering how Dad could possibly have matched this – but he did. The only difference was that Brum got trapped because of a serious blow to the genitals, whereas Dad got a serious blow to the genitals because he got trapped. This most painful of mishaps involved a crowd surge on a stadium staircase. A frantic wave of people ploughed upstairs on either side of a central handrail, but not Dad. No, he cleverly went for the gap in the middle. He was promptly driven straight on to the handrail.

As Mum and friends were carried onwards and upwards in the tide of bodies, they could only look back in wonder at Dad's horrified and pain-racked face as he remained motionless at the foot of the stairs, his privates pinned to a cold metal bar by the weight of a thousand people.

Finally – one last, striking likeness. Brum and Dad, being of pensionable age, like to use their vast wealth of knowledge and experience to embarrass the younger members of their family. This is the way of pensioners.

Although Brum's behaviour one July morning was anything but that expected of a senior citizen. I awoke soon after dawn to the screams and howls of combat. Stumbling half asleep to the window I strained to see through the misty glaze of my contact-lens-deprived eyes. There, on the opposite side of the road, was Brum. He was in a cat fight, and Brum can't fight. As if to emphasise this, his little black opponent suddenly launched forward and sent Brum sprawling whiskers over tail on to his back. A brief skirmish ensued, in which Brum struggled to finish second, and then the screeching, screaming stand-off resumed, with Brum's fur looking rather more dishevelled than it had done moments before. It was clear I was going to have to get him out of this before he got himself killed or, worse, cost me another seven hundred in vet's bills. I raced through the front door and down to the road. Brum's foe spotted me and swiftly departed. Who wouldn't? If a fourteen-stone man in boxer shorts came running at you down a deserted street at 5 a.m., you'd run too.

There was still a problem, however. I wanted Brum inside before his sparring partner returned, but an absolutely livid, spitting, growling, panicked and wound-up Brum still wanted to fight. The said fourteen-stoner in boxers was his only visible target. I made a grab for him but he was too quick – swiping at my hands, falling back on to his hind legs and performing something that looked remarkably like a feline version of the haka. It was quite clear he'd gone temporarily insane. As I warily watched my snarling adversary, the stupidity of the situation hit me – I'd replaced Brum's enemy and now stood fighting with a cat in the street in the early hours of the morning.

I tried clapping my hands in an attempt to drive Brum towards the house, but he was having none of it. He was spoiling for a tear-up and a few claps weren't going to stop him. He bared his teeth. Things were getting serious. I decided the conflict would have to be quick and clinical – I was going for the scruff of his neck and a back leg simultaneously. This technique annoys rather than hurts, and totally immobilises him (don't ask how I first found that out). The key to my success lay in accuracy. I needed to get a grip on him in one swoop or I was going to end up a bloody mess. I crouched low and readied myself to pounce. Brum growled, his ears flattened back and his fur on end.

'OI, TARZAN!' came a sudden shout from nowhere. 'WHAT'S GOING ON OUT THERE? WHAT THE **** DO YOU THINK YOU'RE PLAYING AT? KEEP THE BLOODY NOISE DOWN!'

Both Brum and I looked up in time to see a neighbour's curtain twitch back into place. Tarzan – an excellent if embarrassing analogy given my situation. The man had been treated to the bizarre spectacle of a half-naked man and an enraged cat warily circling one another in the middle of the road. Or jungle clearing. That cat had done it to me again – yet another act of bewildering oddness carried out by the man at number twenty-five. Brum suddenly broke from the fight and ran towards the house. At that very moment, the milkman trundled around the corner in his float.

He blinked twice as he spotted me in the half-light of dawn. Something in my general appearance seemed to upset him. He accelerated past without stopping, all the time trying not to look at me and nervously rubbing his legs. I adjusted my pants and walked solemnly to my door.

Dad's 'humiliating the youngsters' parity with Brum on this one is spot-on.

Dad was in a furniture shop entertaining two luckless grand-daughters. As a good grandfather, he feels it only right and proper that he should behave like a complete moron for his grandchildren's pleasure, and on this occasion was pretending that a wardrobe was a lift and that he was the lift attendant.

Climbing inside, he chuckled 'Going up' at them and closed the door. His granddaughters looked at one another and sidled away to watch from a distance, thoroughly embarrassed by it all. They were immediately replaced by a shop assistant and an elderly couple, who ambled over to admire the wardrobe.

The wardrobe doors suddenly sprang open to a shout of 'FOURTH FLOOR!' and the shocking sight of a manically waving man inside. The couple clutched at their hearts. Dad's surprise was on a par with theirs.

Three horrified senior citizens stared at each other aghast for a few breathless moments before Dad regained his senses and went for the 'sensible' option, darting past them and legging it for freedom, closely tailed by an angry shop assistant, who honestly believed Dad had jumped out of a wardrobe at two unsuspecting fellow pensioners through sheer malice. Two red-faced little girls melted silently into the background.

My dad is getting on a bit now, of course, and a bit old for all these shenanigans, so I'm doing my best to take the baton and carry on the worthy work.

Early promise has blossomed into thirty-something veteran brilliance and I find that every day, in every way, I'm getting worse and worse. I'll soon be there.

Gazebo!

'Heroes have an infinite capacity for stupidity.
Thus are legends born.'

Anonymous

Today was the day!

As Autumn arrived I decided it was finally time to address the gazebo issue. This four-by-three-metre opened-sided tent had been intended to keep our patio in shade throughout the hot summer months, thus protecting Maya and Brum from sunburn. It would now be unlikely to protect them from much more than gently falling leaves, but it was still going up. The gazebo had now become far more than a gazebo. It had become a major bone of contention, and its erection would be a vital weapon in the 'war on nagging'.

As with most self-construction flat-pack items, the assembly instructions were an exercise in disinformation. I truly believe these pamphlets are written by ex-KGB agents who can't quite click out of 'deceive and disorientate' mode. Having broken their code with Sammy's Enigma machine and sat Maya down for an episode of *JoJo the Clown* (should I need any big-top construction tips later), I set about connecting a series of interlocking metal poles. Slowly a huge skeletal framework formed about me. Or fell about me mainly. The poles were all slightly too short. Every time I connected one, another fell out three metres behind me. Brum sat on the garden wall throughout, gazing down at me, ears pinned back in annoyance at each falling pole's metallic clang.

Finally, although aware that the precariously connected poles were not exactly rock solid, I hauled a large fitted cover over the bars. Having shrouded myself three times, it eventually slipped into place and, at last, I stood proudly inspecting the new white roof above my head. I stopped for a moment and smiled at the twitchy-eared silhouette of my tabby friend as he washed atop his wall, clearly visible through the thin fabric

covering. All that remained now was to properly secure that covering to the poles.

My smile broadened as I thought about all the gazebo-conversation-free nights ahead. And then my smile turned to a grimace. The silhouette was doing something it really didn't want to be doing. Its backside was raised and wiggling, its nose pointed straight towards me. Grimace turned to total dismay. The stupid idiot was about to leap down on to the white surface that had suddenly appeared before him. Why hadn't I thought of this possibility? Stretched tight over the bars, it looked to Brum like a perfectly solid, new and exciting roof. Brum's elongated jump preparation routine gave me a little time, but not enough.

As I lurched across the patio yelling 'STOPPPPPPP!' everything seemed to go into slo-mo. I raised a helpless hand to the sky as the shadow of an airborne cat drifted across the white canvas above me. The feline shadow loomed larger and landing-paws stretched forward – and then the world went pear shaped. The unsecured roof caved in about my ears, poles clattered around my feet and a gazebo-cloaked loony-cat smacked into my face.

All this seemed to annoy Brum. I found myself embroiled in a fist fight with a three-by-four-metre white sheet as we both fought to free ourselves (and give each other a couple of slaps in the process). Amid all the chaos I heard Maya screaming something about JoJo having been really naughty with some custard, but I had little time to think about that as ripping sounds now joined the general cacophony of clanging poles, miaowing cat and swearing gazebo builder. A claw dug into my right shoulder

– he was through. My wild and pained left-hand lunge sent my screeching attacker flying.

Suddenly everything was still. Maya mumbled something and was gone – this sort of thing being entirely normal in her recent experience. It will be difficult in later years to explain that everything she learnt as a child about how parents and cats should behave was based on the study of seriously abnormal role models.

I sat in absolute dejection beneath my sheet, my gazebo palace collapsed about me. There was a scratching noise and a corner lifted. A scruffy tabby face appeared and looked at me. I stared back for a few moments and smiled, despite myself. With a bit of determined straining and squirming, Brum forced his way fully inside our makeshift tent and made his way towards me, a look of worried concern on his face. Now I began laughing. He pushed onward through folds of fabric, climbed on to my lap and began purring.

And that was that. A man and cat at peace with one another again, beneath a three-by-four-metre white sheet amid the ruins of an almost-gazebo.

Weird Pets

'Cats, no less liquid than their shadows.'

A.S.J. Tessimond

I'm always getting told pet ghost stories in the pub these days. Ever since asking for them a while back, they're thrust upon me whether I like it or not.

The majority are wind-ups. There is a chill in the air as the storyteller sets the scene and then, just as you're waiting for the shocking finale, they'll scream 'MIAOW' in your ear and you'll choke on your peanuts.

A really silly story concerning Brandy, the shy tortoiseshell, is a good example of a typical wind-up. Brandy wasn't just a little shy, she was painfully shy. Unfortunately her owner was a real party animal and filled her house with guests virtually every night. Not only that, she'd dress Brandy up in ribbons and bows, parading her at parties like a show poodle.

Brandy died on a party night, killed while trying, as normal, to hide from a house full of noisy people. She'd hidden under a car in the drive just as its owner was the first to leave. At the moment of Brandy's demise, her owner had an overwhelming sense that something terrible had happened. She swore she'd seen Brandy's face in her mind and that Brandy was trying to tell her something. That night, she saw Brandy again, in a harrowing dream. Brandy was dressed in party clothes, walking around on her hind legs in a bizarrely human way. Suddenly Brandy turned and hissed at her, accusing her of ruining her short life and swearing to haunt all future parties at the house for evermore, hiding from every guest that entered her home. The owner woke in a sweat, her ears ringing with Brandy's last words. And, as unlikely as Brandy's claim may have seemed, it should be noted that since her death, almost four years ago . . . Brandy's ghost has never been seen.

You see what I have to contend with.

But every now and then I get a cracker. This was told to me by a girl whose parents owned a huge black cat back in the 1970s. Blackie (names weren't a challenging thing back then, were they?) had been a bit of a pain around the house, and regularly got on the wrong side of the girl's father. His worst habit was ripping the father's suit trousers to shreds. Now, while ripping things up is a fairly normal feline activity, it can get pretty expensive when it's good-quality work suits which are being destroyed at a rate of one per month. Everybody loved Blackie except the fed-up father, and the fed-up father decided Blackie had to go.

Blackie had been with the family for years and really didn't want to leave. He was sent to live with a relative on the south coast, which was nice as the family could still see him now and then. Alas, they never did. Within a week of moving he fell seriously ill and a couple of days later he was dead. The really sad thing was that, if the family had known it was coming, he could at least have died in his own home.

But (of course) that wasn't the end of Blackie's story. A few weeks later the father was woken by scratching noises. He investigated, finding nothing, but as he turned the light off he saw the silhouette of a cat sitting on the chair at the end of his bed. He hurriedly switched the light back on and stared long and hard at an empty chair. In the morning he'd virtually forgotten the incident – until he pulled on his suit trousers. Both legs hung in tatters, torn to pieces. He'd bought the suit only a day before. Purr-fect feline revenge, I think.

At about the time Blackie was busily destroying suits, other ghostly happenings were occurring in the very next street, although this particular story has a rather different ending. A couple, friends of my parents, in fact, had recently said a sad farewell to their old tabby, who, in keeping with the imaginative naming policy of the era, was called Tabby. Tabby had been ill for some time and was eventually put to sleep a few days before the couple's summer vacation. They set off for Spain, hoping a couple of weeks in the sun would help lift their spirits, and left the house in charge of a young friend, who, having no property of her own and residing with relatives, eagerly agreed to house-sit and feed the couple's rabbits, goldfish and tortoise.

The house-sitter was surprised on arrival at the house to find there was also a tabby that needed feeding. She was well aware the couple had just lost a cat, but assumed they must have had two and forgotten to mention the second. She soon located a bowl and a good supply of cat food in a cupboard, so just got on with her job. She couldn't help noting, though, that the cat had rather erratic behavioural patterns, always appearing nervous and distant, vanishing for long periods, sometimes for two or three days. Some evenings it would sit in a chair and stare at her for hours – never sleeping, just staring. It was all a little unnerving, but the house-sitter assumed that the tabby was just missing its owners and couldn't get used to a stranger in the house.

When the couple arrived home they were shocked to see Tabby's old food bowl back in use and an open tin of cat food in the fridge. A note, left by the house-sitter, filled them in on all the gossip they'd missed, thanked them for the use of their house and, in a startling footnote, mocked them for forgetting to mention there was a cat to feed.

They immediately phoned the house-sitter, as you would, and asked the basic but burning question, 'What cat!'

The house-sitter gave a chillingly accurate description of Tabby. It was difficult to gauge who was more shaken – the couple who'd just been informed that their deceased cat had returned from the grave, or the poor house-sitter, who suddenly realised she'd spent two weeks sharing a house with a ghost.

The story could have ended there, and Tabby would've forever been remembered as the cat that had risen from the dead. But that night came one final twist. As the couple settled down to watch TV, they heard the cat-flap spring open. They looked at one another in alarm and hurried to the kitchen. There, standing in the middle of the room, was Tabby. Or at least a tabby. Not their Tabby.

Not a ghostly visitation at all, but a neighbourhood chancer who happened to wander through an inviting cat-flap at just the right moment, finding a young girl who immediately prepared him a meal and made him a welcome guest for two whole weeks!

Much more ghostly than this is the story of the recurring white cat. This goes way back to the 1950s and is pretty weird. The white cat in question was named – wait for it – Whitey . . . no, not really – the cat's name was Billy.

Billy belonged to a member of the fire service and his owner tended to move from town to town, station to station, on a regular basis. Billy lived for only three years, long enough to move home twice. Shortly after arriving at his third home, he was hit by a car and died. Around a year later, the fireman moved on again. He'd been in his new home a week when a stray white cat appeared on the doorstep. The fireman took him in, just as he had Billy. They were friends for only a short while. This cat too was killed in a road accident.

It was two years before the fireman relocated again, and waiting on his doorstep at his new house was a stray white cat. The fireman was beginning to find things strange. The cats were all different but all of them, Billy included, had come to him when he'd moved to a new home. All had behaved in roughly the same manner, had the same habits and, sadly, all died in the same way. The third, like Billy and his successor, was killed by a car.

The fireman moved again, almost expecting a white cat to join him. No white cat appeared and the fireman felt a pang of remorse – maybe it was finally over. It wasn't. Six months later a stray white cat came to the door. It was the absolute spitting image of Billy, now dead for over seven years. The fireman named him Billy, swearing that he really was Billy and telling friends that he'd recognise him anywhere. An old black-and-white photo proved there was indeed an uncanny resemblance. This Billy survived, and seemed to have learnt from old mistakes. He was terrified of cars, and never once set foot beyond his owner's drive.

Strange, that one.

So would this one be, if it didn't involve my sister, Sarah. I reported in Brum's first book that Sarah's daughter, in her young days, had an uncanny perceptiveness about ghostly goings-on. She claimed, at two years old, to have been visited by a cat who died before she was born, giving an accurate description of the cat in question. The cat was Brum's brother, Lester, and the reason I bring the subject back up is that Lester is claimed to have visited recently.

Sarah has only one cat these days, a wild little white-and-marmalade named Leon (Leigh-on-Sea). Leon now possesses a clever habit of getting stuck in very high places and has become a popular figure with Beaconsfield Fire Brigade. Way, way up an extremely tall tree at dusk one evening, he began his usual 'I'm stuck' wailing.

Sarah sighed a sigh of repetitive resignation and took up position at the bottom of the tree, beginning her 'coaxing down' routine (biscuit-box-rattling and screaming abuse). After five minutes she noticed Leon wasn't alone. Sitting next to him, too far away to see clearly in the failing light, was a small silver-grey tabby. Sarah squinted and strained to see. Being a rational, clear-thinking type of girl, Sarah instantly assumed the tabby to be Brum's long-dead brother and gasped in disbelief. Well, not disbelief, but belief actually – total belief in anything and everything. She rushed inside to find binoculars. By the time she returned, the light had virtually gone and all she could make out was the rough shape of the two cats, high above her. One began to make its way tentatively down, half skipping, half falling from branch to branch.

As it reached the lower branches, Sarah could see it was Leon. She looked up high again. The other cat was gone. She looked and looked, but no other cat became visible.

As a ghost story, the incident can obviously be discounted owing to the anything-goes spiritual credibility of its only witness, but I still believe Lester appeared to the crazy witness's daughter and wonder whether, spiritual sensitivity often running in families, Maya might possess the trait. Early signs, however, are that like me she has a complete lack of facility (unlike me, only when it comes to the world of spirits).

Not only does she not seem to perceive any 'presences' at all, she steadfastly refuses to accept the existence of Santa Claus and laughs out loud at any mention of monsters, ghosts and tooth fairies.

Even when we left a particularly harrowing computer game, involving the blowing to pieces of corpses and zombies, on the screen (as all good parents do), she merrily danced back into the living room yelling, 'THE HOUSE . . . OF THE DEAD' in deeply disturbing tones.

No, it's only the dinosaurs which worry her, and they, after all, did actually exist. Being too young to appreciate that sixty-five million years is a long time to have been dead, she just won't accept that the dinosaurs' extinction is a definite conclusion. She feels we've made a mistake on that one. But if Maya has no special qualities in making contact with the spirit world, she's certainly managed to emulate her father in making contact with the world of the weird. In her choice of pets, that is.

She's just acquired two goldfish (in a frenzy of Nemo-mania) who are particularly weird but, having spent her whole time on earth with Brum, she probably expected nothing less. Brum wasn't *my* first pet, of course. And not the first weird one either. Oh no. When I was very young I had a hamster called Carling, named for my father's use of a pub ashtray as a water bowl.

Carling looked OK, but he was as mad as a lorry. Why else would he spend all day every day standing beside his exercise wheel, turning it with one paw? Not *in* his exercise wheel, exercising, but just idly flicking the wheel round and round, round and round, all day long, every waking hour.

Did he somehow believe that the wheel *had* to be turned, and that he'd found a 'minimum effort, maximum gain' method of hamstering? Did he perhaps think that his turning the wheel provided the world with electricity? And then, one day, he got even weirder. He lost his front left leg. How do you *lose* your leg? One day he had it, the next it was gone. He wasn't bleeding or anything, he was just one leg short. Even Brum hasn't achieved anything on that level . . . yet. I've little doubt that he will. I'm quite sure that some day he'll hop home with an appendage or two unaccountably missing. It didn't seem to bother Carling in the slightest, but one effect of his dramatic limb loss was that he was no longer able to turn the wheel.

With no interest in running inside it, the wheel remained still for the rest of his days, which just so happened to be the very same days of the 1970s when the country became plagued with constant electrical power cuts. You now know why those cuts occurred. Absolutely nothing to do with trade unions, everything to do with a small rodent named after a plastic ashtray.

Maya's new goldfish are hopefully not destined to bring Britain's national grid down, but they are a little odd. Or at least, I think they are. I'm not exactly sure what fish are meant to do so I have no idea whether staring at a big gormless tabby face all day long is normal behaviour. But that's what they do. I always thought fish lived in a little world of their own, predominantly ignoring the world beyond their tank, but Bob and Dad (Maya's choice of fish names – Bob is a good one as that's what he does all day, but Dad? Lorraine thinks maybe she recognises something in that gormless open-mouthed look) seem to have built up an instant rapport with Brum. They all stare at each other for hours, as if communicating on a telekinetic level. Either that, or all three of them are as thick as two short planks and can't think of anything better to do.

Back to ghosts and, leaving the most ridiculous until last, for sheer spooky stupidity this one has to come top. If this snippet of a story is true, as the teller swears it is, then it's proof indeed that reckless incompetence goes on long after the last breath is drawn. Brum will be very at home in the afterlife.

The teller had a cat who liked to climb aerials. His death was crazy. He climbed to the very top of a rooftop radio mast, bending it over with his weight. It bent so far over that its tip almost reached back down to the roof. The cat spotted this as a convenient place to dismount and stretched two paws on to the tiles. The removal of over half his body weight twanged the aerial upright at breakneck speed, catapulting the cat into the air by his hind legs, off the roof and straight into the road. A passing driver, probably not expecting a cat to fall from the sky, careered off the road and hit a tree.

The cat was dead on the scene. The car driver survived. The spooky thing is that, ever since, the road has suffered from epidemics of unexplain-able TV and radio interference. Could it be that this moronic cat, not content with killing himself in a vain bid to silence Terry Wogan, was still up there, hanging off antennae and blocking the airwaves? No doubt in my mind. Or my sister's.

There's one last eerie footnote to all this. My grandfather was still in the fire service during the 1950s, despite not enjoying the 1940s one little bit (a bit heavy on the old aerial push-biking opportunities), and it is from him that we heard the story of Billy, the recurring white cat.

In fact, my grandfather knew the final Billy very well. So well, in fact, that he took him in when his owner tragically died on duty in 1959.

The records grow dim here and my grandparents are no longer around to ask, but just who, exactly, was the white cat named Billy I clearly recall them owning in the late 1980s . . . ?

The Carpet-fitters

'He that is down need fear no fall.'

John Bunyan

With one freestyle-vomiting champion cat, one hunter-killer moggy and one food-chucking toddler, we tend to get through carpets. The carpet-fitters were coming again.

Really and truly, I should be fitting our carpets myself. I trained as a carpet-fitter upon leaving school, something that turned out to be a pretty bad career choice in all truth. During sixteen years of practical schooling, I proved beyond doubt that I was totally incapable of cutting anything in a straight line. It mattered not a jot whether I was trying to cut paper, wood, metal, fabric or simply a dashing figure, everything meandered off in wildly ridiculous arcs (especially the dashing figure). This sort of thing isn't a good trait in a carpet-fitter.

Fortunately, once actively training to be something I didn't have any hope of ever being, I very rarely managed to get my Stanley-knife blade anywhere near expensive rolls of carpet – its only real function being the daily slashing of my hands and knees. Similarly, my hammer's purpose appeared to be securing my fingers to lengths of multi-nailed gripper rod.

My long-suffering and often blood-splattered boss finally managed to persuade me to leave by refusing to pay me any more money and suggesting I took up an apprenticeship with a local electrician. Looking back, I do wonder whether he was trying to get rid of me in more ways than one. Surely a lad who somehow managed to turn carpet-fitting into a highly dangerous activity would without doubt kill himself when dealing with high-voltage electricity? I think he wanted to make absolutely certain I'd never work for him again. Not even as a favour.

Knowing my track record and the danger I represented, an

electrician still took me on. I believe this was less a case of him giving me a second chance, and more a case of him being a lunatic.

I wasn't an electrician for long. By the time I met Brum, I'd thankfully said goodbye to all that, sacked for my dismal job-to-explosion ratio. My next job involved smashing holes in walls. It was a job I proved exceptional at and still do well to this day, albeit unintentionally. But I still like to tinker in the trades, still like to ruin the odd carpet, ignite the odd appliance. One particular tinkering jumps immediately to mind . . . It was a bright spring morning, and I awoke with a strong urge to fit an outdoor socket – as you do. I had all the right equipment, all the right tools and a sketchy idea of what I was supposed to do.

Brum watched[*] my tinkering with the air of a devout fan. He sat on my car bonnet in the drive, yawning as if cheering as I ran back and forth from house to drive, wire trailing everywhere. He observed every single move I made, his eyes following me for the best part of an hour, not wanting to miss a thing. He looked delighted the whole time, his face set in a big happy smile, and when I reached the finale – the wiring in of the socket itself – he wandered over to offer his congratulations.

Somewhere between in and out, up and down, back and forth, I'd managed to switch the power back on and forgotten to switch it off. Therefore, as I confidently grabbed a live wire between finger and thumb I received a nasty electric shock, which was something I'd become fairly used to during my electrical apprenticeship and so no massive problem. However, I don't know if you know, but a secondary electric shock is much worse than an initial one. Touch somebody who's got 240 volts coursing through their body and you're in big trouble.

And so it was that I acted as super-conductor for my super-tabby. An eagerly sniffing feline nose connected with my arm at precisely the wrong moment and was suddenly airborne, along with its owner. Brum must have thought the world had gone crazy again.

---

[*] Brum's 'industrial watching' technique always proves rather poor. A little too 'paws-on'.

He brushes his face against his owner's arm and suddenly there're sparks, explosions and he's hurtling backwards into a fence at ninety miles an hour.

He hit that fence so hard that three fence panels smashed in half and he rebounded back two feet into the drive. Somehow he just got back up, every charged hair standing on end, and walked back towards me as if nothing had happened.

He reached me, sniffed my arm again (which must be about the most stupid thing it would be possible to do in the circumstances), seemed deliriously happy that the arm in question hadn't served him another star-bursting hammer-blow to the face, and settled down, purring.

For reasons now obvious, Lorraine stopped me messing with 'practical things' and, despite my still being keen to fit our new carpet, felt much safer paying somebody else to do it.

As she pointed out – there's still every chance my electrics will burn the house down and so it's important that no badly fitted carpets bunch up against doors and restrict fire-brigade access. 'Jack of all trades, master of my own demise,' she called me, and then chuckled to herself for nearly half an hour (ha bloody ha). We're making her odd, Brum and I. She never used to be like this.

My cause faltering in the face of Lorraine's 'wit', I was finally silenced forever by a raised hand and the mouthed word 'gazebo'. I flinched, glanced at the mangled and ripped wreckage that still lay bundled in a corner of the patio, and rang the carpet-fitters.

Had I known the entertainment they would provide, however, I'd have willingly paid double. In fact, the cabaret started before they even arrived. Our fitting contract stipulated that 'the customer should completely empty the room and remove any existing carpet'. Probably a better wording would have been: 'the customer and his toddler should work against one another and completely fail to empty the room or remove any existing carpet and cat' (forgive me for saying 'cat' rather than 'cats' here, but Sammy doesn't involve herself in matters of the workforce).

Owing to this contractual wording oversight, I totally underestimated the time it would take to empty a room, which was mainly why I started the task thirty minutes before the carpet-fitters were due to arrive. The house very quickly descended into chaos. While Sammy slept soundly in the farthest room, I knocked pictures from walls and chipped paint from doors as I slowly but steadily piled the contents of the lounge in the kitchen. Brum took up his normal 'loud activity' pose – standing right in the middle of the action with his hair on end, a mixture of astonishment and panic in his eyes.

Not once did he think to move. Not once did it cross his mind to go to another, safer, room. Consequently I spent the best part of half an hour stepping on him, tripping over him, dropping things on his head and accidentally booting him across the room. If I tried to move him aside with a gentle push he fell over sideways.

As I marched back and forth with items, so too did Maya. It took me quite a while to realise she was moving items in the opposite direction, refilling the living room as fast as I emptied it. With these two lending their assistance, it was quite a relief to reach the final item – the three-seater sofa.

After I'd raised my end and watched Maya grunt for a few moments at hers without anything much happening, I tipped the sofa up on its end, so that one arm rested on the floor and the other almost touched the ceiling. At this point I noticed a gaping hole in the fabric on its underside, and a sharp spring poking out. Great – a new sofa required[*] too. It took me a few minutes to

---

[*]Maya has acknowledged this need for replacement seating in song. Her favourite record to date has been 'Friday On My Mind', and she has somehow transmuted one of this song's most famous lines into 'Daddy's eating all the fishes – yeah, he'll change settees some day'.

bend the spring back inside and trap it against other dodgy springs, and then I was ready to go. My aim was to walk the sofa on its end, shuffling it as I went, towards the door, and then tip it through.

Things went very well. With a huge grunt I messed up totally, sending it toppling straight back down into the space it originally occupied, and which now unfortunately had been taken up by a curiously sniffing Brum. All I could do was clasp my hands to my head as it fell, expecting Brum's familiar shriek of hurt surprise at any moment.

It never came. I thought I'd squashed him. I dropped to my knees and lifted the edge of the chair. Either he was as flat as a pancake, or he'd gone.

How on earth had he got out in time? He needed to have moved like a turbo-charged cheetah. Brum can't move like that. And not only had he avoided the sofa, he'd somehow darted past Maya before she'd had time to mount him and ride him 'rodeo' down the hall. Impossible.

I shrugged and whipped the sofa end up to the ceiling again. There was a loud dull thud and *now* the Brum shriek. I jumped in surprise and looked all around the sofa. No Brum. Baffled, I dropped it back down. There was another shriek. I stared at the sofa and glanced around the room, but there was absolutely no sign of him. Realisation began slowly to dawn. It dawned with an element of 'surely not'. Could he really be inside the sofa?

Then I heard loud scratching, and the scratching had an echo. I looked at the sofa again. No doubt about it – the noise was coming from inside. I quickly flung one end high into the air again, a rather reckless action which brought forth another crash and shriek. I studied the exposed underside of the sofa and the huge gaping hole adjacent to my face. I poked my face into the hole. From six feet below, in the inky blackness of the sofa's hollow base, came a deeply irritated miaow.

I couldn't quite believe it. He hadn't got out of the way at all. Of course he hadn't. He simply stood still and watched the sofa land on him. By sheer chance, the hole came down exactly where he stood and swallowed him. Brum, being Brum, accepted his new surroundings instantly and without question, and set off to explore the sudden dark cave, continuing until blindly thumping into its opposite end. Then the cave shot into the air and sent him crashing from one end to the other.

Typically, at this moment, with the carpet still down, the sofa on its end and Brum trapped inside, the doorbell rang. The carpet-fitters had arrived – an old chap and a lad of about seventeen.

They marched in and looked at the almost cleared room while I busily explained that my cat was stuck inside the sofa. I had the distinct impression that they weren't listening to a word I was saying. I'm not sure they even noticed I was speaking. Without breaking stride and with one abrupt push, the older man sent the sofa crashing back to the floor. Then they grabbed an end each and marched back towards the door. They didn't get far.

A bedraggled-looking cat dropped from the sofa's underside like a stone, providing an unexpected hurdle to the young lad whose legs were taken clean from under him. The lad stumbled forward, pushing his boss to the floor and slamming the sofa down on his chest. Brum, for good measure, jumped on to the sofa and began washing.

Judging by the boss's expression, the lad was in big trouble. A great deal of silent animosity followed as the pair resumed their room clearance, dumping the sofa in the hall and completely ignoring the blissfully content cat on its middle cushion. As they began ripping up the old carpet, it occurred to me that they hadn't said a single word. Not to me, not to each other, not to Brum or Maya. I asked whether they wanted a drink The old chap shook his head, the lad nodded, the old chap glared at the lad and the lad shook his head. Not a word. Skilful stuff.

They soon shot back outside and appeared moments later with the new carpet, marching on into the living room without stopping. I was about to speak when they slammed the door in my face. A few seconds later the door swung open, Maya hurried out and it slammed behind her.

For the next fifteen minutes there was a great deal of crashing, banging, shuffling and grunting. I didn't know quite what to do with myself. I paced up and down the hall for a while, as if they were delivering a baby rather than fitting a carpet. Maya followed me up and down, attached to my shirt-tail. Twenty minutes later came the first spoken word, and it was a fine one.

'BOLLOCKS!'

Followed swiftly by 'SHIT!'

Then the soaring finale: 'SOD IT! BOLLOCKS! BUGGER'S UNDER IT, BUGGER'S UNDER IT!'

There was a great deal more crashing, thumping and shuffling. The door opened. Brum hurtled out with his tail between his legs and ran for all he was worth. The door slammed behind him.

I hadn't even realised he was in there. Was he the 'bugger under it'?

I knocked on the door. The thumping and shuffling stopped abruptly. There was silence for a full minute and then it all started again. Bump, shuffle, crash, thump. They never replied.

On about the half-hour mark, there was a sudden burst of bewildering conversation.

'Civil War,' said the old one.

'What?' said the lad.

'American Civil War.'

'What American civil war?'

'What? What American civil war? *The* American Civil War. The flipping American one.'

And that was it. Not another word, just crashes and thumps.

Ten minutes later, they marched back out. I said, 'Are you done?' but they were gone. By the time I got to the front door, they were getting back in their van.

'Excuse me,' I shouted. I had to know a couple of things.

The lad looked up at me.

'What happened with the cat? What did the cat do?'

The lad looked stunned. He climbed quickly into the van and the van sped off.

I felt as if I'd been subjected to a hit-and-run carpet-fitting

179

raid. It was as if they'd been in an unoccupied house. They seemed scarcely to perceive my existence at all.

I walked back inside. Brum and Maya had wandered into the lounge to inspect the carpet, and both were rolling around on it. I smiled at the daft tabby lying on his back, his front paws straight up in the air as if he'd just been shot.

I'll never know exactly what happened, but I can pretty much assume they must have dumped the new carpet straight on top of him and started fitting it. The only surprise is that they didn't fit it around him and leave a cat-shaped lump in the middle of the floor.

There's something else I'd really like to know too – what on earth was the American Civil War bit about? Nothing in that room could've prompted the sudden, seemingly out-of-the-blue comment 'Civil War'.

All I can do with that one is put forward my theory, and here it is:

The carpet-fitters, working towards a huge bonus, have somehow learnt to bend space-time. This was the reason my presence was largely superficial to them. I was like a dull groan in the background.[*] As they buzzed back and forth through time, they were moving at impossible speeds that made me appear to be merely a stationary object.

At some moment, their temporal-shifting carpet-fitting techniques went awry, and the old boy felt the need to comment that they were passing through the American Civil War. Once the lad had clarified exactly which American civil war his boss was referring to, he made the necessary adjustments and brought them away from the thunder of cannon and shrieking rebel yells – and back into twenty-first-century High Wycombe.

It was shortly after postulating this theory that I realised staying at home with Maya and Brum was, without doubt, driving me insane.

---

[*]Many people think of me as a dull groan in the background.

Death Threats

'*Diplomacy is to do and say,*
The nastiest thing
In the nicest way.'

Isaac Goldberg

Possibly the nicest promise Maya has ever made to Brum could in some ways be perceived as an extremely unnerving threat.

Delivered with a broad smile, head cocked to one side in disarming, loving friendship, stroking the edgy-looking Brum's head, 'I won't kill you, Brummy' could be taken in a number of ways.

First and foremost, it could be taken purely at face value. From this we'd ascertain one thing and one thing only – that Maya won't kill Brum. Which is good. She was merely reassuring him of the fact. What is perhaps more worrying is why. It's not the sort of thing you say to someone, is it?

I don't go up to people at work, put my hand on their shoulder and soothingly assure them I have no intention of killing them. If I did, I'm sure the last thing they'd take away from the exchange would be that I was safe to be around. For a start, they'd be seriously worrying why the thought was in my head in the first place. Second, having never, before that moment, suspected that I might want to kill them, they'd have to seriously re-examine my attitude towards them. Their only conclusion would have to be that I'd seriously considered the option.

When I actually do some work, I work with market researchers. Therefore, yes, I admit I would have to seriously consider the option of killing my colleagues.

So, the second reason for Maya's warm gesture may have been a dark one. She'd been harbouring murderous thoughts and felt the need to reassure herself rather than her tabby. By the worried look on Brum's face, this reason may well have occurred to him. If this is the true reason for her comment, at least it shows that she's fighting the urge and so very unlikely to carry it out. The third and worst reason, and the one I believe most likely, is that it's all a poker bluff, and she's going to kill him.

And if I need to discover a motive, it's staring me in the face right now. In fact Brum is staring me in the face right now, and that's enough motive for anyone, but also – Maya is mad.

And it's not just Maya. All toddlers are mad. They run around in circles making blabbering noises, seem to be stoned and drunk the whole time and find excitement in every little thing (Maya actually cheers if you turn a torch on). They are totally off their trolleys, all of them, but Maya has also recently displayed some rather macabre personality traits that send shivers down my spine and which Brum should take very careful note of.

I think the first sign was when I found Homer Simpson's head missing. My talking Homer alarm clock has been beside the bed for years and I only ever look at it when it tells me it's time to get up. On this particular morning I responded to the shout of 'BUT I GOT UP YESTERDAY!' by, as usual, attempting to punch Homer in the face, only to find his face inexplicably missing.

When Maya wandered into the bedroom, clutching her Winnie-the-Pooh handbag, she looked a picture of butter-wouldn't-melt innocence. When I asked her whether she knew anything about my headless alarm clock, she smiled, unzipped her bag and pulled out Homer's head. Still smiling, a little manically, she said that she wanted to keep it in her bag . . . always and for ever. Where on earth did she get the idea to do a thing like that? Somebody carrying a decapitated head around in their handbag is surely the sort of thing you'd read about in a James Herbert or a Stephen King, not in *Bob the Builder and the Frozen Duck Pond*.

A day or two later, I caught her trying to shove Brum into the tumble dryer. Now I was getting really worried. My theory was gaining momentum.

As if the headless Homer business wasn't enough, she then displayed incredible violence towards Bill the Flowerpot Man. When I found him, it was too late. He lay in Maya's potty and, after what had happened to him, the only thing he'd be seeing would be the inside of a body . . . er, bin bag. The one coherent thing that toy ever said was 'WEED'. How ironic.

I had a long chat with Maya about this, for the obvious reason that you don't put toys in your potty. Maya may be noisy and criminally insane, but she *is* obedient. That's why Bill's best mate Ben met his own near-identical fate in the toilet. There's a difference between the potty and the toilet, you know.

And then, as if to emphasise the thought processes going on in her mind, the first question she asked me when I picked her up from a toddler friend's birthday party was, 'If you're dead, you're in the ground, eh, Daddy?'

Chilling. And it was obviously something she'd been dealing with at the party. Is that the sort of subject that comes up when you throw a bunch of toddlers into the same room? Do they talk about burials all day long? Are they all plotting to murder their cats? Or is it more an innocent case of the infinite-monkeys theory – put enough monkeys in front of typewriters for an infinite length of time and eventually, inevitably, they will write the complete works of Shakespeare? In other words, could it be that toddlers talk so much non-stop nonsense that they're just bound to get around to murder eventually?

Because of all this, I became increasingly suspicious of her. She could sense my unease, and became equally suspicious of me. Every time I moved, her little eyes followed me like a hawk's. Every time I left the room, she demanded to know what I was doing. Because I didn't want this to be the prevailing atmosphere between us, I put the subject out of my mind. But then I heard her on the phone, asking Gandalf Stick for 'monies'. When he refused, probably because he was one hundred miles away and wasn't about to wire her bank account, she said, 'Then I huff, and I puff, and I blow your house down!'

Her first protection racket. Surely the message to be taken from the story of the three pigs is one of hard work and good materials, not one of extorting money from elderly people through threats of damage to property.

I continued to push suspicions of her tendencies to the back of my mind, but then she started making seriously derisory comments about Brum. He'd always been her favourite, so where did this come from:

'Mummy, Sammy's very pretty, isn't she?'

'Yes, Maya, she is. Do you think Brum's pretty too?'

'No . . . he's just OK.'

Although (understandably, I suppose) she's had much the same sort of conversation about me. 'Mummy, you're beautiful, aren't you?' (Pronounced more like bewley-sul, but we knew what she meant).

'Yes, I am [Lorraine doesn't mess when it comes to self-promotion]. And you're beautiful too.'

'Thank you, Mummy . . . Mummy?'

'Yes, Maya.'

'Where did we get Daddy?'

Charming.

And although this story centres on the utterly stupid premise that Maya would do away with her feline friend, I must admit for a horrible moment that it looked as if my fears were well founded.

Maya came running to me one day, her eyes full of tears, and blurted out the shocking words:

'I really sorry to Brum. I got him dead. I really sorry.'

'What, Brum, dead, now, how?' I blurted back.

'I was hitting Piglet with him, and he got dead.'

Avoiding the urge to correct her grammar and explain she had in fact been hitting Brum with Piglet and not the other way round, I followed her into the living room to find Brum crumpled in a heap in the corner. Piglet's legs were poking out from under his midriff.

I have no idea how Brum came to be on top, and the evidence *did* seem to point to Maya's grammar being correct after all, but he looked to be in urgent need of medical assistance. Predictably, when I tried to offer some, he bit me.

So, I don't know what happened in that room, but if it was a murder attempt it failed – Piglet is still very much with us. As is Brum.

And I'd always thought Maya wouldn't want to hurt anyone! She says she likes everybody, you see (another clever toddler ruse?). Absolutely everybody. No matter who they are and no matter how they behave, Maya says she likes them. She's diplomacy personified. But if you're really astute and learn to read between the lines a little, you very occasionally discover her true feelings about a person. Not surprisingly, I've only achieved this feat once, and it concerned Maya's cousin Anna. Anna became jealous about Maya dancing with her little brother at a family party and didn't behave in a friendly way towards her at all.

On the way home in the car, Maya composed and performed a song in honour of Anna that could be taken either way:

> I like you Anna
> Come on, dance with me
> I like you Anna
> Come on, dance with me
> You're as clever as mouse's feet
> And you don't scare dogs away.

A few months later, I asked how clever mouse's feet are.

'Not very clever at all,' Maya replied.

Epilogue

'The hard part of being a bartender is figuring out who is drunk and who is just stupid.'

Richard Braunstein

A nd in the winter, Brum died.

We buried him beneath the bramble bush he used to tangle himself in, and stood at his graveside as the first sprinkling of snow settled on the grass.

Lorraine and Maya went inside and I stared at the fresh earth for a long time.

Eventually, as the evening grew cold, I whispered a quiet thank you for that last summer, and followed them in . . .

. . . or at least, I would have done. Had he been dead.

No, he hasn't died at all. Sorry about that. It would've made a poignant ending to the book, but the above is merely the lead-in to a fantasy chat-with-the-cat.

So, Brum's funeral has just taken place, we'll carry on from there . . .

I follow them in, but slip on the icy steps, do two somersaults and go straight over the twenty-foot wall . . .

The setting: a weird 'afterlife'-style foggy, surreal room that looks remarkably like a pub lounge bar.

CP: Good evening, Brum.
BRUM: Well, I wasn't expecting to see you here.
CP: No. Well, you would have to go and pop your cork on the first 'icy-steps' day of the year, wouldn't you.
BRUM: Well, I'm sorry if my dying has inconvenienced you in some way.
CP: Inconvenienced me? Inconvenienced me? It killed me!
BRUM: Ah well, that's life. You never get out of it alive, do you?

CP: Hmm, anyway, it's nice to be able to talk to you. Gives us a chance to catch up on all the old gossip and that.

BRUM: Couldn't you have devised some cat-speak microchip? Killing us for a chinwag at the end of every book you write is a bit drastic, don't you think?

CP: Why do you always do that?

BRUM: What?

CP: Criticise everything I say and do?

BRUM: What are you talking about? I'm a cat. How on earth have I been 'criticising' you?

CP: I've seen those condescending looks. You spent half your life sitting around looking at me in that smug way of yours.

BRUM: Oh, that! I had to do that. Cat rule number two – always stare condescendingly at humans and yawn in a bored kind of way if they attempt conversation with you.

CP: What's rule number one?

BRUM: Vomit on their bed.

CP: Are there many cat rules?

BRUM: Oh yes, loads. Four, in fact.

CP: Four? What are the other two?

BRUM: Rule three states that a cat must always behave with extreme poise, elegance and dignity in every undertaking.

CP: Had trouble with that one, did you?

BRUM: Not really.

CP: Slipping off roofs and half drowning in paddling pools is dignified, is it?

BRUM: Rule four is to never, absolutely never, do anything anybody ever tells you to do.

CP: So?

BRUM: I applied it to rule three.

CP: Ah, well done, smart thinking. So, rule four explains why cats won't allow themselves to be trained like dogs, does it?

BRUM: Sort of. But that's as much to do with dogs being big slobbery crawlers who'll do anything for a filthy old bone and a rub behind the ear.

CP: Bitter little fur-ball, aren't you? You'd never see a cat helping out the human race like dogs do, though. You don't see cats guiding blind people. You'd be more likely to trip them.

BRUM: True. Where is this place, anyway?

CP: It's a pub.

BRUM: A pub?

CP: Yes . . . you know . . . a pub.

BRUM: What, as in the place you were always going to or coming back from? So this is a pub. Why are we in a pub?

CP: Well, one thing I'd have really liked to have done during our lifetimes was go down the pub and have a few pints with you.

BRUM: Why?

CP: Well . . . I don't know . . . pub with your mates. It's a sociable thing to do, really.

BRUM: No, no. Why a few pints? I don't drink 'pints'. I drink in sips . . .

CP: Slurps.

BRUM: Slurps?

CP: You drink in slurps. Not sips. You're a disgusting drinker.

BRUM: Me! At least I don't guzzle down whole 'pints'. What stupid creature other than a human would drink its own blood volume in one sitting? It's a good job you people stand on two legs. Your bellies would hit the floor if you had to walk on all fours.

CP: Maybe that's it, Brum! Maybe that's why we ended up bipedal . . .

BRUM: So you could drink more beer?

CP: Yes!

BRUM: You live in your own little world, don't you?

CP: Well, yes, I suppose I do. But everyone knows me here.

BRUM: Actually, thinking about it, you end up on all fours after a few beers anyway – I had to nudge your face out of my food bowl once. That rather blows your theory, doesn't it?

CP: Alright, alright. Cats don't drink pints. Humans drink

too much. Fine. But I'd have liked to have had a beer with you. That's all.

BRUM: And I repeat . . . why?

CP: Because you seemed half cut your whole life anyway. I wanted to see if beer would make the blindest bit of difference.

BRUM: But I didn't like beer. You made me try it, and I hated it.

CP: I didn't make you. I offered you a sip of mine.

BRUM: I think you'll find you shoved my head in the glass.

CP: I was just trying to get you to sniff it. As I remember it, you got pretty vicious about the whole thing.

BRUM: So would you if someone shoved *your* head in something foul – my cat food, for instance. Anyway, beer is stupid. It's just another human frailty. I wouldn't touch a drop of the stuff if my whole life depended on it.

CP: You're dead. Would you like a beer?

BRUM: Yes please.

CP: Pint?

BRUM: Yes please.

A ghostly dog barman delivers the drinks.

BRUM: (*whispers*) Why's the barman a dog?

CP: I don't know.

BRUM: What?! This is *your* fantasy. Surely you have some idea, some tiny little inkling, why the barman would be an upright dog in a waistcoat and bow tie?

Both stare across at the ghostly dog, who is now busily cleaning glasses.

CP: I *really* don't know, Brum. I don't remember thinking that character up at all.

BRUM: Well . . . have you ever been in a pub and been served by a dog? Ever?

CP: No . . . oh, hang on, I think I see where that came from. Better drop the subject.

BRUM: Do you think he heard my 'big slobbery crawler' remark?

CP: Don't think so. But I'd keep your voice down if I were you.

BRUM: HE'S GOT BIG HORRIBLE YELLOW TEETH, HASN'T HE?

CP: Just drink your pint and keep quiet.

BRUM: SLURP! SLURP! SLURP! BELCH! PURRR!

CP: You're putting that beer back fast, boy.

BRUM: SLURP! Stop watching me like that. You're always watching me and writing things on your little notepads. Don't think I haven't noticed. Weirdo.

CP: Brilliant. Now my cat's calling me a weirdo. Criticism, criticism, critiscism.

BRUM: YOUR cat? Here we go again. I'm 'yours', am I?

CP: Well . . . yes.

BRUM: Who went out to work and who lay in bed all day? Who provided food and who ate it? I'm not yours . . . you're mine! SLURP!

CP: Slow down with the beer.

BRUM: And another thing . . . I still don't see why you have to kill me off at the end. You've written two books and I end up dead in both of them. That's not nice, is it?

CP: It's not personal.

BRUM: Killing someone once could be deemed accidental. Killing them twice is personal. How did I die, anyway?

CP: In a terrible fireball accident.

BRUM: Bloody Nora. That's a bit much, isn't it? Couldn't I just have passed away quietly in my sleep?

CP: No.

BRUM: No?

CP: No. All summer I waited for you to self-immolate. You used to do it all the time. I had my notebook in my pocket for four months, and not once did you bother catching fire. I was determined we'd have a combusting-cat incident at some stage in this book . . . so now we have one.

BRUM: But a ball of fire! What a terrible way to go. I hope you'll reconsider this.

CP: I can't. It's already written.

BRUM: What, written in the stars or something?

CP: No. I wrote it just then. A few lines back.

BRUM: BURP HAH!

CP: Another beer?

BRUM: Yes please. Don't be so stupid. Just edit it out.

CP: I can't. I'm dead. It's out of my hands.

Ghostly dog delivers new drinks. Brum shifts uneasily on his seat.

BRUM: (*whispers*) I still don't understand why it has to be a bloody dog? Why do I have to put up with all this nonsense? I'm writing to Tabby Rights, or the RAC or whatever it's called. They'll have something to say about you fireballing me to death and sending me to a dog-pub.

CP: RSPCA.

BRUM: Yes, them. I'm writing to them . . . I think . . . What does RSPCA stand for? The white cat speaks highly of them.

CP: Respecting Spontaneously Pyromaniacal Cat Accidents.

BRUM: What?

CP: It does!

BRUM: Really?

CP: No.

BRUM: (*ears-back frown*).

CP: Anyway, you know why we're here, so let's get started.

BRUM: We're here because we're dead, owner o'mine. Not a good time to be starting anything much . . . You know, I like beer. Beer is my friend.

CP: Now come on, I wanted to talk about the summer we've just spent together. I'd like your views and opinions, all that old rubbish.

BRUM: My views and opinions are rubbish, are they?

CP: Yes. No. I mean, I don't know yet. I expect so.

BRUM: OK. Let's get on with it. Go ahead, punk, make my day.

CP: I was a punk, funnily enough.

BRUM: (*silence*).

CP: Way back before you were a twinkle in your moggy mother's eye, I was strutting about in ripped-up bin-liner tops and listening to the Clash and the Pistols at full blast on my first hi-fi system.

BRUM: (*silence*).

CP: I was only twelve years old. I knew all the swear words and I . . .

BRUM: Is all this by way of telling me you're an idiot?

CP: You were a bit of a punk when you were a kitten.

BRUM: I was a punk?

CP: Yep. I was still playing the music when you moved in. You used to sit with your head touching the speaker and purring. You loved it.

BRUM: I don't remember liking your music at all. Are you sure I wasn't trying to deafen myself?

CP: You did like it! And you danced. You were a right head-banger.

BRUM: Really?

CP: I'm not sure, actually. You certainly seemed to love head-banging . . . although a lot of that was forgetting to duck when you walked under coffee tables.

BRUM: You wanted to talk about the summer?

CP: Yes. First of all, how well do you feel you've coped with the . . .

BRUM: BURP HAH PURRR.

CP: (*Sigh*) Another one?

Brum silently waves glass.

CP: I knew you'd be good at drinking.

BRUM: Why?

CP: I don't know really . . . alcohol made me look like a pillock so many times in my life. Beer offers this sort of scope for disaster that's almost impossible to match. Looking back, I think you'd have to be a complete moron to drink to excess, so . . . I suppose I'm amazed you weren't an alcoholic.

BRUM: HIC!

CP: Now I'm dead, I wonder why I was as fond of the beer as I was.

BRUM: Ish bloody great.

CP: Hmm, OK. Anyway, back to my question. How well do you feel you coped with the little'un this summer?

BRUM: Oh, really, really well. It's taken a long while, but we're almost friends now. I think she's great, and I think she likes me . . . it's hard to say because she's always hitting me.

CP: That's really nice, I thought you two got on OK. I know she got upset about the bedroom and the paddling pool and that, but mainly you got on fine, didn't you?

BRUM: Bedroom? Paddling pool? No problems with those as far as I remember. No, we got on well. Even went out for walks together, that sort of thing.

CP: Out for walks? No you didn't.

BRUM: Yes we did, loads of times. HICCUP.

CP: Brum, I was with her the whole time. You didn't, absolutely didn't, go out for 'loads of walks' together.

BRUM: You were with her the whole time? Don't be so stupid. She doesn't even like you.

CP: Now, Brum, that's a cruel thing to say. She's my daughter so she has to like me. That's the law.

BRUM: But it's true. And we did go for walks. We even hunted together . . . hang on . . . WHAT! The white cat's your *daughter*? How on earth did that happen?

CP: Not Sammy! I'm talking about Maya. Since when has Sammy been 'the little'un'? She's not even slightly little!

BRUM: She's smaller than me.

CP: No she's not! She's huge. Just how big do you think you are?

BRUM: I was sure I was bigger than her . . . it must be because I see me closer up.

CP: Oh dear. So, you got on well with Sammy, then? How about Maya?

BRUM: Maya, yes, the big-headed one. She's OK. Bit bad tempered, but OK.

CP: You know, talking of offspring brings to mind a question I've always wanted to ask you, something that I've never known. Did you ever have any kittens?

BRUM: SPISHHHHPLAT.

CP: Oh, for pity's sake! Have you been sick? That's gone all down my bloody shirt.

BRUM: No, no, cough, sorry, cough, hang on . . . cough, I'll be alright in a minute.

CP: You just spat your beer all over me. Why did you *do* that, Brum?

BRUM: Cough. Sorry. The question just caught me by surprishe.

CP: What – did you ever have any kittens? Why? And are you slurring?

BRUM: No, I'm not. And (*giggles*) I thought you knew I was a tomcat.

CP: What? Of course I knew . . . oh, grow up, will you. Did you ever *father* any kittens?

BRUM: I think so. Back at the flat, before . . .

CP: Before . . . ?

BRUM: I still reshent that, you know?

CP: (*grimacing*) Oh. That. I can understand that, Brum. Sorry. If someone had taken me down the vet's and . . . anyway, let's just say I'd be a bit more than resentful.

BRUM: That Commissioner Herbert (*emits involuntary hiss*), was it . . . him?

CP: Yes, it was. You obviously didn't like him either, then?

BRUM: Well, I certainly don't now.

CP: No.

BRUM: Yes, well. Before . . . that, I think I fathered thousands.

CP: Thousands?

BRUM: Thousands. There were a lot of cats around those flats, and I was a bit of a shtud in those days.

CP: No more beer, OK? No more boasting, beer-fuelled, super-stud nonsense. Did you have any kittens?

BRUM: One litter, I reckon. The boy looked a lot like me.

CP: Just one definite kitten, then. I wonder what happened to him.

BRUM: No, five kittens. It was a litter. HIC.

CP: Ah, but their mother was super-fecund. Didn't you know that?

BRUM: How dare you suggest she was shuperfu, shuperf, shupe . . . does that mean what I think it means?

CP: No, no, it's not a nasty word at all. It just means that she could have been with any number of men and she . . .

BRUM: WHAT!

CP: No, no, let me carry on. There were loads of local tomcats and she could've had kittens by quite a few of them, all in the same . . .

BRUM: THAT'S IT, MATE, DON'T YOU MESS WITH ME WHEN I'VE BEEN DRINKING.

CP: Oh no, you're not going to ask me outside again, are you?

BRUM: YES, I . . . nah, let's just have another beer. I like you, you're my besht mate, you are, Chris, and you are too, dog. I love dogs (*lifts paw and wipes tears from eyes*).

CP: I knew you'd had too many. No way I'll get any sense out of you now. Typical. What do you want to do when the pub closes, then? Go for a catnip kebab or head down the tandoori – I think they've served me cat food once or twice.

BRUM: I know what we can do . . . we're ghosts, right?

CP: Yes?

BRUM: Let's go and haunt Commisshhhioner Herbert!

CP: For once, Brum, we are in total and utter agreement.

Paw and hand meet in a high-five as cat and owner leave the bar.

A *few hours later, in a dimly lit veterinary clinic in High Wycombe, absolutely nothing happens.*